PRE-EXISTENCE OF MAN

Parts I and II Combined

by

Hilton Hotema

THE BOOK TREE
San Diego, California

First published
1960
in two separate volumes by
Health Research
Mokelumne Hill, CA
USA

Additional material and revisions
© 2020
The Book Tree

ISBN 978-1-58509-399-1

Cover art
©
Bruce Rolff

Published by
The Book Tree
San Diego, CA
www.thebooktree.com
We provide fascinating and educational products to help
awaken the public to new ideas and
information that would not be available otherwise.
Call 1 (800) 700-8733 for our *FREE BOOK TREE CATALOG*.

INTRODUCTION

This book begins with a brief summary of mankind's knowledge within all of the major scientific fields, which is impressive in itself, but then moves forward to explain why this great knowledge falls short. Science explains the processes of life and what we know of its origins and mechanisms. However, the author brings this knowledge to another level by explaining how a pre-existent, spiritual structure exists as a foundation for our scientific knowledge. What he presents is what is missing in our pursuit toward a complete understanding of life on this planet, including human life itself. We are shown how the processes of life on Earth involve the movement of all elements and life itself from the invisible realms into the visible and back again, in an eternal process of construction and destruction. This explains the wonders of Creation, which mankind has been pondering for centuries. According to the author, you, the reader, would never have come into this physical existence unless you had previously been in the invisible world first. He explains how this power exists within ourselves, and that we may one day tap into it when we are ready. Woven into the fabric of this book is ancient knowledge, reintroduced in order to remind us of the spiritual truths that we have lost.

Not only does this book reveal this ancient knowledge, it shows exactly how the Western World lost this wisdom of the ancients and how Christianity was born. It explains how the priesthood of Rome created a New Religion in the fourth century, which became Christianity as we know it today. The author claims that this religion is, in large part, based on legends of gods from India, Egypt, Greece, and Asia Minor, with much of the ancient knowledge having been intentionally destroyed or assimilated into the Bible itself. According to the author, much of the story of Jesus is sourced from a Greek historian named Damis-which only a few serious scholars seem to be aware of. The work of Damis centers largely around his master Apollonius, who had taught and preserved a great deal of the ancient knowledge. This book does a great job in explaining the lost wisdom of the ancients. One is sure to come away from this book with a more complete understanding of human life and our true place in the universe. This Book Tree edition includes parts one and two together, which were originally published separately.

Paul Tice

CONTENTS

PLEASE NOTE: Contents for Part II appears on page 25.

L I F E

If a man die, shall he live again? Is Life temporal or eternal? (Job. 14:14; 2 Cor. 4:16).

For these burning questions the church and modern science have no answer. Science knows no more now about Life than it did a thousand years ago.

Science has explored Life down to a single cell of living matter, but what makes the cell alive is a mystery to science.

The great cosmic ray scientist Millikan wrote: "I cannot explain why I am alive rather than dead. Physiologists can tell me much about the mechanical and chemical processes of my body, but why I am alive they cannot say." (Collier's, Oct. 24, 1925.)

It is interesting and enlightening to review scientific speculation on this question.

Bichat opened his celebrated "Recherches Physiologiques sur la Vie et is Mort" by defining Life as "The sum of the functions by which death is resisted."

That tells nothing and is just a circuitous way of asserting that Life is nothing more than the ability, quality, and property of being able to live. Or to resist "death," which implies that "death" is an entity, a demon, constantly waiting for a chance to destroy Life.

Fletcher defined Life as: "Life consists in the sum of the characteristic actions of organized beings, performed in virtue of a specific susceptibility, acted upon by specific stimuli."

To Fletcher, Life was just the body's activity. Richerand said the same in these words: "Life consists in the aggregate of those phenomena which manifest themselves in succession for a limited time in organized beings."

Now comes the renowned Osler, greatest physician that America ever preduced, and he "scientifically" defined Life in these words: "Life is the expression of a series of chemical changes" (Mod. Med. 1907, p. 39).

Osler did not define Life. Like all the rest, he merely described the processes of Life.

If the term Life simply means the attestations of its processes and presence, the signs of Life and nothing more, these great scientists have done about as well as the subject permits.

Prof. Le Conte took a turn at the puzzle. Listen to what he said:

"In all cases, vital (Life) Force is produced by decomposition. Whence do animals derive their vital (Life) Force? I answer, from the decomposition of their food and tissues." (Conservation of Energy, pp. 175, 188.)

According to this wild theory, Life rises from decaying matter. From stinking, rotting vegetables and animal flesh there comes forth the exalted principle called Life.

That mysterious, unlimited, eternal Force, which forms plants, animals, and man, and endows them with various powers, that gives man an intellect by which he could raise himself far above the low level to which his mis-education and controlled mind have reduced him,--that potent force is "produced by decomposition." So says science.

It is unbelievable to think of serious minded scientists presenting and espousing such a preposterous proposition.

That is what our children get in the schools and colleges. That is the shoddy bill of goods being sold to the masses in newspapers and over radio and television in the catchy slogan: "Better schools build better communities."

It required centuries of careful scheming to fix the educational institutions of the world so that each rising generation would be trained to run in the rut prepared by those who live and thrive on the ignorance of the deceived masses.

BIOLOGY

The noted astronomer J. B. S. Haldane said: "We are at present almost completely ignorant of biology, a fact that often escapes the notice of biologists.

Haldane shows that science has no law of biology, no law of psychology, no law of physiology. He inveighed against "the belief that biology will consist merely in physical and chemical discoveries as applied to man, animals, and plants" (Daedalus, p. 50).

He opposes the theory that science can reduce Life to a mere physical and chemical basis. He believes that Life is more than "the expression of a series of chemical changes."

Dr. Robert Walter said: "Chemical Affinity, under control of Vital (Life) Force, works constructively. But as soon as Vital (Life) Force departs, the same Chemical Affinity works destructively and destroys what it previously aided in building up. Vital (Life) Force, being the highest order of force known, employs in its service all agencies beneath it; but it neither falls to the level of its servants nor lifts them up to its own level." (Vital Science, p. 187.)

The great Carrel also opposed the chemical theory of Life. He declared that Life is more than physics and chemistry. He said that while the laws of mechanics, physics, and chemistry are applicable to inert matter, they are not to man. Then he shouted:

"The illusions of the mechanicists of the 19th Century, the dogmas of Jacques Loeb, and the childish-physico-chemical-conceptions of man, in which most physiologists and physicians still believe, have to be definitely abandoned." (Man The Unknown, p. 108). Then he quickly added:

"How naive our speculations! Our knowledge of the human body is, in truth, most rudimentary. It is impossible, for the present, to grasp its constitution (p. 109).

That frank confession by a truly great scientist of modern times shows how silly and stupid it is for us to look to modern science for help and guidance in our search for Light.

NATURE OF LIFE

Biologists vie with one another in confessing their ignorance of the Nature of Life.

Biology cannot pose as a science as long as its leading lights confess ignorance as to the Nature of Life.

Biology consists almost entirely of nothing but a description of the phenomena and conditions of Life. The Nature of Life itself, biologists declare, is unknown to them.

That is erroneous. The Nature of Life is known and understood by its work, but material science stubbornly refuses to admit it. Man is cognizant of the Nature of Life by observation, experience, and consciousness.

We live, we are alive, therefore the Nature of Life is known.

POTENTIAL BEING

The Masters said that the center of Light is the Supreme Being. In their words, the Supreme Being united with Sophis (Wisdom) and communicated to it The Germ of Transformation, and the Material world was the result.

The Masters held that the Immaterial (Spiritual) Structure exists before the Material--the theory of Archetypes of Telearche.

Accordingly, Thought Forms, Pre-existence, Potential Being, visible image of the invisible Eternal, emanating from Cosmic Mind as the activating Germ, unfolded as Man (evolution), clothed in the garment of the Cosmos, corresponding in color, number, and vibration to the Solar System as it is at the moment of the beginning of the transformation of the Invisible Man to the Visible Man.

-3-

Dr. Gustaf Stromberg, noted astronomer, presents in "The Soul of the Universe" a theory of creative processes which he demonstrated to be sound and correct. He begins with the Circle and makes his theory harmonize with cosmic principles.

The Ancient Masters used a Circle to symbolize the Creative Center. They knew that creative processes work in circles. The products are circles. The Universe is composed of circles. Man's body is composed of circles. The body cells are circles, composed of circular atoms, which is composed of electrons that are circles and move in circles.

The atom is composed of an orbit of electrons revolving round the nucleus in its center as the planets revolve round the Sun. The electron is a center of whirling force and revolves round the nucleus, the central sun in the atom.

ELECTRICAL FIELDS

Stromberg asserted that "In the living world there are organizing fields (composed of whirling centers of force), which determine the structure and functions of living organisms.

These fields are definite and well defined. They expand during embryonic development, attain full size at maturity, and, at death, the Ego that inhabited the organized form, the body, contracts to a point and vanishes in the astral (invisible) world.

Stromberg demonstrated the theory of potential being to be a fact. He showed by experiments that an immaterial, invisible, pre-existing form is back of every material form, back of every cell,--a theory presented by Lakhovsky. When the cell is what we call dead, that immaterial form lives on. He wrote:

"The structure and functions of a cell, a nerve system, a brain, are not due to the collected molecules of the cells, but to an electrical field with definite properties, structural as well as functional."

He experimentally studied the electrical field to see if there were any around a tadpole. With an exceedingly sensitive electrical instrument he explored the electrical field in the water surrounding the tadpole. When the animal was undergoing metamorphosis, changing from tadpole to frog, the effect was startling.

He found, to his amazement, that the structure of the future animal was already in existence as an immaterial (spiritual) form before it had acquired or changed to a material substratum. The form was there before the pattern wherein the molecules had become incorporated in the material form.

Stromberg said, "The substance, which was the Soul in the solution, clicked into place, and (presto changeo) an animal came into physical being."

Carrel wrote, "An organ develops by (mysterious) means, such as those attributed to fairies in the tales told to children....It cannot be explained in the light of our present concepts" (Man the Unknown, pp. 107-8.)

The immaterial, spiritual structure, the Potential Being, not only comes first and exists first, but it lives on and remains after the material form has disintegrated and disappeared. Not only in the case of man, but of every living thing.

THE ZODIAC

The ancient Zodiac, a map of the starry sky, is an imprint of the physical sheaths of man's body and indicates, like a clock, the plane of Will and Consciousness in which Solar (Soul) Forces works thru the body.

Man, the peak of all creation, greatest of all creators, contains within himself all the potential powers, systems, planets, and globes of the universe. The body cells are composed of atoms; and the atom is a tiny universe in itself.

Man's body is a mass of millions of suns, stars, planets, organized into systems of cells, molecules, atoms and electrons, all whirling in the body at terrific speed, producing great power which is the power of the body; and that power emanates from the electrical fields described by Stromberg, and these fields are emanations from the mighty Sun, the God of the Ancient Masters, who said: "For our God is a Consuming Fire" (Heb. 12:29).

Man, the Microcosm, is the image of the Macrocosm (Gen. 1:27). The Masters said, "That which is above is like that which is below."

Man embodies the Seven Planes of Being: (1) electronic, (2) atomic, (3) molecular, (4) cellular, (5) organic, (6) Human, and (7) Divine.

COSMIC CYCLE

All things and elements move in circles, from the invisible to the Visible and back again, in the eternal process of construction and destruction, of integration and disintegration. That work is called Creation, but the more correct term is Transformation, Things are transformations not creations.

Littlefield writes, "All visible forms have their counterpart (pattern) in the invisible world." (p. 180).

He holds that the visible world is a materialization of Cosmic Thought Forms existing in the Spiritual World. Thought Forms are the origin of all living things on earth (Way of Life, p. 76).

He further says that living forms are entirely dependent upon the Life Principle, the living form being only an expression of the Life Principle, not productive of it (p. 359).

The Masters taught that what appears as the Life Principle rises from the effect of Solar Electricity, generated by the Sun, acting on the positive and negative poles of the invisible atoms of which all living forms are constituted.

"The Sun animates all things. Ani is the Sun; Ani-ma is the Life; Ani-mare means to animate," wrote Dunlap.

The Law of Thought Forms, existing in the Invisible World, was expressed by the Masters in these words: Every plant of the field (was in the air) before it was in the earth, and every herb of the field (was in the air) before it grew. (Gen. 2:5).

The church fathers, without doubt, omitted men from the Law or Potential Existence when they copied, edited, and distorted the ancient literature for their Bible.

SOLAR RADIATION

LIFE is not a chemical function nor a physical factor, as claimed by science.

LIFE did not originate in the sea, nor come from a single cell, as claimed by evolutionism.

LIFE is a Cosmic Principle that emanates from the mighty Sun. It charges the air and flows thru the air, hence the Ancient Masters termed it the Breath of Life, while Paul wrote: "For Our God is a Consuming Fire" (Gen. 2:7; Heb. 12:29).

The Bible further says, "A fire goeth before him (the Sun) and burneth up his enemies round about him. His lightenings enlighten the world. The earth saw, and trembled. The hills melted like wax at the presence of the Lord (Sun)" (Ps. 97:3-5).

Solar Radiation makes possible radio, radar, and television. It is the mysterious substance of the atom with its terrific power.

See the flowers of the field follow the glorious Sun. In the morning, the Sun Flower is facing east, and in the evening it faces the west. The Nature of Life is known, but material science refuses to admit it.

If the mighty Sun would fail, the earth would sink in total darkness, would be as barren as a rock, and the gods of all races and all times would be utterly helpless and useless. The gods need the Sun, but the Sun needs no gods.

Solar Force, Solar Radiation, Solar Electricity, call it what you will, acts on inert matter; and thru organized forms it manifests certain and definite mental, emotional, volitional, and sensational qualities that are not chemical nor physical and are different in every species of animal and plant.

This is conclusive evidence to show that One Life animates all living

-6-

things and that the organized form, not the Life Principle, governs the character of the manifestations.

The time will come when these material biologists must take due cognizance of the Psychic and the Mental as well as the Physical and Chemical Principles.

The psychic qualities of Life in animals and man are never fully apparent. They lie in wait, as it were, for the opportunities and occasions of expression. They are there and ready to act when the conditions for action are present and appropriate.

When external and internal circumstances are suited to the expression of the Psychic Qualities of Life, the expression responds, is called forth from the mysterious realm of the unseen.

This Primal Law of Expression accounts for the first appearance of living forms on the cooling surface of the young earth.

THE GOD MAN

Life is an omnipotent force, a cosmic principle, a phase of Solar Radiation; and when conditions become suitable for living forms to appear, then the primal bacteria, fungi, and protozos naturally came from the invisible realm, to be followed in due order by all the higher species from amoeba to man, each entity being a presentation, as it were, from the astromental region of the universe above the physical plane.

The theory of evolution, the idea that higher species ascended from the lower, is an impossibility on the face of it.

That which is superior is invented and superadded to that which is inferior. The superior nature of man is invented and superadded to the inferior anthropoid nature--according to the theory of evolution.

Man is a person, and his personality developed by increments of Mind and Emotion that result from his superior brain development.

Cosmic processes produced the personality, and the superior Mind, the result of a superior brain, have endowed that personality with mental faculties, emotions, and ideals far above the nature of other animals.

In possessing the Cosmic Power of Creation, man is a creator in his own right. He is a free agent, an independent creature, and is responsible for his own conduct.

Man is the God of his own being and existence. He has within himself the power of propagation and perpetuity. He can never become extinct. His pre-existence is plainly evident.

Nor were there magic powers given to men or bestowed upon him by some imaginary god. They are an inherent part of him, of his very being, and cannot be given to him nor taken from him.

Man has within himself all the potentialities of his own existence. He is the only true God. That God dwells in man and man in him, as the Bible says. And they are on the earth, not in the sky, not in "that home above."

The Bible says, "Know ye not that your body is the Temple of the Holy Ghost, which is you?"...Know ye not that ye are the Temple of God, and that the Spirit of God dwelleth in you?" (1 Cor. 3:16; 6:19).

No effort of concentration nor degree of reflection, no matter how long continued, can make man conscious of a personal identity in himself that is not himself--that is separate from his body and distinct from his own brain.

That fact is conclusive evidence to convince a rational mind that the Spirit of God, said to be dwelling in man's body, is none other than Man himself.

Man could not come into the visible world if he did not exist in the invisible (spiritual) world.

It is axiomatic that something cannot come from nothing, regardless of what the church says, or what it made its god say.

In harmony with cosmic law, occult science holds that actual existence rises from potential existence; that physical existence is the materialization of spiritual existence.

Under the Law of Cosmic Radiation, physical man appears as the materialization of his spiritual duplicate. Man's visible form is a replica of his invisible frame, says Prof. Lakhovsky.

Clear, invisible light is an example of Potential Existence. In that clear light there exist all the various colors of the rainbow, and they materialize and become visible when proper conditions are supplied.

Likewise the invisible frame of man, under proper conditions, materializes into a visible form.

That is Transformation, and not creation as the church sells it.

Under the Cosmic Law of Being, man could not be the God of the visible world if he were not the God of the Invisible World. Man would have to be the Ged of the Invisible World in order to become the God of the Visible World.

That is the reason why the Ancient Masters said that "the kingdom of God is within you" (Lu. 17:21). That is literally true. It is not just a figure of speech.

Man is supreme over all institutions and not they over him. He has natural empire and dominion over all things and institutions. They are for him not he for them. But the church, for profit and power, has reversed this natural law and order.

These facts appear simple, and all intelligent men should assent. But man is not easily convinced of the truth. For the subtle intellect of the professional schemer can weave his mist over the clearest vision.

Man is the only God the world will ever have, find, or discover, and Man is an Eternal Being in his own right.

True Being is not the result of organization but the cause of it. It is not an aggregate of modes of motion, nor a succession of phenomena and perceptions, but the cause of them.

True Being is a Living Spirit, a Spark of the Great Central Light that enters into and dwells in the body to be separated therefrom in the process called death and return to its original source.

True Being is an independent state of eternal existence. It does not disperse nor end at death, like breath or smoke, nor can it be annihilated. It still exists after the death of the body as it existed before the birth of the body.

CREATION--TRANSFORMATION

Creative processes are really transformative processes.

What is called creation is the transformation of potential existence into actual existence, spiritual existence into physical existence. The process had no beginning and has no end. It is in constant and eternal operation.

The starting point on the physical plane is the atom. It contains twelve particles and a nucleus of solar electricity.

The nucleus at the center activates the atom, and the aggregation of atoms produces form.

The twelve particles consist of six positive and six negative in polarity. The positive revolve clockwise, and the negative, anti-clockwise.

These particles are powered by the attraction (positive) and repulsion (negative) of the nucleus.

The nucleus of the atom occupies a position analogous to the Sun. The motion of the planets of our solar system is ruled and powered by the attraction and repulsion of solar force, not by so-called gravity as claimed by science.

In their particular timing in their orbits, all twelve particles of the atom contact the central nucleus regularly, to sustain their motion.

Like the Sun, the nucleus, powered by solar electricity, possesses infinite power, and power can be drawn from it indefinitely.

The atom is a miniature universe, and the nucleus corresponds to the solar center of the universe. The work of each is creative, transformative, and the power of each is infinite.

Principles of Existence

The causes of things are the Principles of Existence, and these Principles operate according to law and order.

Every Principle of Operation is an Invisible Force and has an unchanging order of work. The force, being recognized by the mind, becomes a Principle of Science, which produces, governs, and being understood, explains every phenomenon that follows.

Transformative Forces are invisible as the transformative principle in a seed, a bud, a germ, an egg.

Existence is the unfolding, the evolution, of Transformative Principles, which mould the visible things in Nature from the invisible substance of the universe--as invisible gases form water, then ice, and back again to invisible gases.

This order of operation was declared by the Ancient Masters (Rom. 1:20), and confirmed by science, without a possible fact in the universe to controvert it.

The chick is not the development of the visible material of the egg but of an invisible principle of Life that transforms the material to a chick--building from the material an organism that corresponds with the parent organism--from the duck, a duck; from the hen, a chick; but from an infertile egg, explosive gases.

Recognizing this truth, we observe that Like begets Like, each after its kind.

An interior, invisible Principle of Existence is a necessary conclusion of the human intellect and confirmed by the analogies of Nature in every department of existence.

The arguments admitted to sustain this conclusion yield an exactly similar and equally important one, which, though just as logical and certain, may not be so readily admitted, though we cannot see now any thinker can doubt it, viz., that the cause, whether first or last, or anywhere along the line of causes, must be the comprehensive equal of the effect; and, conversely, the effect must be the comprehensive presentation of the cause.

If a millionth portion of an atom can be added to the universe beyond the sufficiency of the cause, there is no reason why the whole universe shall not exist independently of a cause; and if the universe is causeless, all its parts must be equally so, and every principle of science must consequently fail.

If the slightest increase of the effect beyond the sufficiency of the cause can be secured, every relation of Cause and Effect must fail, and not only Science, but the human mind be proved incompetent to any conclusion.

If the cause is not the equal of the effect, then some part of the effect is causeless, and if a part is without a cause, why not the whole?

Consistency of thought demands that we proceed in our processes in a direct course thru infinite time to infinite results.

If dead, decaying matter can produce Life, if unintelligent matter can produce intelligence, if unconscious matter can produce consciousness, and mind, there is no reason why man shall not progress to infinite capacity by virtue of the power residing in the circumstances of his Environment; and if infinite results can be obtained by progress in one direction, we are for the same reason justified in concluding that all visible things come from nothing.

Life only from Life, each after its kind, is the order of organic development.

The facts of observation confirm the deductions of reason and the inferences of analogy, without a fact in the universe to cast any doubt upon the conclusion.

Life is a dynamic, energizing, determining Principle of Existence; and that Life is what? Its work reveals its nature.

Life first shows its presence in protoplasm, indefinite, organless, living matter, which, though alive, is not Life. For we may see dead as well as living protoplasm, proving that Life is an Infinite Force distinct from either.

Though organless, Life produces all organs, as all observers agree, and still it is the fixed and unchangeable order of each after its kind.

Life only from Life; ducks only from ducks; corn only from corn; and man only from man--not man from ape.

Vegetable protoplasm will not produce animals; animal protoplasm will not produce man; the protoplasm of a black man will not produce a white man.

Life, as an indisputable, observed fact, is not the result nor the effect, but the cause of organisms.

Organisms produce protoplasm. Certainly reproduction is one of the great facts of the universe; but reproduction only because of an inherent quality in living things that makes reproduction possible.

Man produces progeny only because he is the product of Life from the Original Source and endowed with the capacity to make reproduction thru him possible.

Be not confused nor misled at this point. Man is not a producer of progeny, though it so appears. We do not see what we think we see.

Man is the product of Life Force and cannot produce what has produced him.

Reproduction, as the term is used and understood, is a myth and a misnomer. Nothing ever reproduces itself.

Living things cannot reproduce what they cannot originally produce. But they are so constituted that they are competent to supply conditions in which the Primal Force of Existence will lay hold of Invisible Elements and mysteriously weave them into various and definite forms, thus transforming Invisible Forms or Patterns into Visible Organisms.

Infinite Source

The Original Source of Living Existence must be recognized as an Infinite Source—infinite in duration, in power, in character, in quality.

The reason that concedes the Original Source to be necessary also concludes that the Original Source shall be the equal of all that follows—the equal of the infinite capacity to which all things tend.

The character of the Original Source is described by the things made as stated by the Ancient Masters (Rom. 1:20).

The lesser can never produce the greater. Progress is the great fact of all ages, but progress beyond the Original Source is an impossibility—a dream of a disordered mind.

Progress will continue thru infinite existence but will never and can never exceed its Source, any more than existence, as we have it, could have some from something infinitely beneath it, and finally, from nothing.

Upward to the cerulean heaven, and not down to the slimy mud at the bottom of the sea, must we look for the origin of living things.

If something cannot come from nothing, then of necessity the something from which things come must be the equal, at least, of all that comes. And that which comes describes with great clearness the character of that from which it comes.

The requirements of human reason necessitates the conclusion that:

1. Every effect indicates a cause;

2. The cause is and must be anterior to the effect;

3. The cause is and must be interior to the effect, as the term evolution suggests;

4. The cause is invisible, a Principle perpetually unfolding to results;

5. The cause must be the efficient and sufficient equal of the effect.

6. The cause must answer to the requirements of all things just as each subordinate cause does to its effect.

7. Conscious Being, the highest order of all existence, must rise from the Original Source and be illustrated by all such processes as necessarily are inherent in Mind.

Cross of Life

The exoteric fail to comprehend biblical symbolism because it has an esoteric meaning that finds explanation only in Cosmic Laws.

Each cell of the body is bipolar, has a nucleus of solar electricity, and is dominated by magnetic force.

The polar properties of attraction and repulsion are very marked. Cells unite and separate exactly as do two electrified bodies, showing that the cells are charged with electricity.

The cell expresses two other functions, viz., volition and sensation.

These four fundamental functions of Life, of the body cell, which modern science fails to notice, result from the action of solar radiation on the poles of the cell, producing all phenomena called Life, with each organ and gland of the body performing its allotted work.

And the endless search for a mysterious Life Principle goes on and on, because the searchers ignore the Nature of Life and know not for what they are searching.

Let us imagine an upright bar with negative and positive poles. To this upright bar we affix a cross bar with volition and senation poles.

The Ancient Masters termed this the Cross of Life. This ancient symbol presents a clear picture of the four phases of solar radiation in relation to the human body.

Three salts, phosphates of lime, magnesia, and potash, will give ex-

-13-

pression to solar radiation as Life, and build the Cross of Life, each of the four points of which give expression to each of the four phases of so-called vital force.

The Cross of Life may be built experimentally by the same combination of phosphates of lime, magnesia, and potash as found in the body cells, thru which Solar Radiation manifests the four functions mentioned.

Transformative processes exhibit these four fundamental functions of Life, which inheres in the atom and appears in the body cells.

Without these four fundamental functions, there would be no creation, no transformation, no universe, no organized forms, no Life.

Cosmic Intelligence

Modern science has somewhat discovered the power of the atom, and the magnitude of that power shocks the world.

Science lags far behind the Ancient Masters in its failure to recognize the INTELLIGENCE of the atom.

Atomic Intelligence rules the vegetable kingdom. For instance, if trees are watered in dry weather, their roots will turn up toward the surface of the ground for that water but will go deeper down for moisture if not watered. This conduct shows that atoms know their work and how to do it.

Carrel declared that the "existence of Intelligence is a primary datum of observation" (Man the Unknown, p. 121). Then he cited an example of the work of Cosmic Intelligence. He wrote:

"Isolated cells have the singular power of reproducing, without direction or purpose, the edifices characterizing each organ. If a few red blood corpuscles, impelled by gravity, flow from a drop of blood placed in liquid plasma and form a tiny stream, banks are soon built up. These banks then cover themselves with filaments of fibrin, forming a tube, thru which the red cells glide just as in a blood vessel" (p. 107).

Cosmic intelligence is exhibited in the work of the atom. The aggregation of atoms produces cells; and cosmic intelligence is exhibited in the work of the cells of the body; but that intelligence is intensified with all the combined power of all the atoms in the cell.

The aggregation of cells produces organs; organs from the body and cosmic intelligence appears in the body as biologic, psychologic, and physiologic intelligence, rising from the atom, intensified with the combined power of all the atoms in the body and producing what we call the unconscious or subconscious Mind, lying beyond the reach of the will-power of the five senses.

From the subconscious Mind rises the Conscious Mind, appearing as man's sense powers, and being Cosmic Intelligence manifesting thru the brain in Man's three-dimensional world.

Book With Seven Seals

Revelation, last book of the Bible, deals with the psychic phase of Cosmic Intelligence, which is a manifestation beyond the power of the common five senses, and raises man to the fourth dimensional plane of being.

Super-consciousness, a rare state found in the cases of true clairvoyance, is a union of the power of the conscious and the subconscious phases of Mind.

Due to the thorough manner in which the scheming church fathers destroyed all ancient literature in order to hide their fraudulent work, it has taken many ages to discover that the original Scroll of the last book of the Bible came from India.

Kundalini Yoga teaches all about the Book with Seven Seals. The book represents man's body; and the Seven Seals represent the seven major nerve centers of the body.

The Lamb, standing in the midst of the throne and looking like it had been sacrificed (Rev. 5:6), does not represent the gospel Jesus as the stupid clergy think, but the Candidate who has been tried, tested, and accepted for initiation in the Ancient Mysteries, where he will be taught how to open the Seals of his body and activate the sixth and seventh sense powers of his brain, as so well explained by Kismonti in his remarkable work titled "Awaken The World Within."

That greatest teacher and magician of the first century, who later became the Jesus and the Paul of the New Testament, went to India about the year 36 AD, was initiated in the Hindu Mysteries, and given the Scroll that became a part of the Christian Bible.

In baffling symbol and allegory, the Scroll described the strange effects that man experiences when he follows the Regenerate Life taught in the secret work of Masters.

When this renowned teacher returned to Asia Minor, his native land, he retired to the isle of Patmos and spent considerable time there revising and editing the Scroll to make the context harmonize with the conditions of his country and the customs of his people. The work was titled the Apocalypse, a Greek term that means "disrobing" or "unveiling," and hence translated Revelation in the Bible—but revealing nothing but confusion to the exoteric.

The Bible

As this Scroll, Revelation, appears in the Bible, it is filled with spurious interpolations and clever distortions. It begins with the false statement:

"<u>The Revelation of Jesus Christ, which God gave unto him</u>." etc.

We shall cite an example to show how skillfully the cunning compilers of the Bible distorted the ancient scriptures:

Correctly translated from the Greek, this passage reads: "<u>For the evidence of resurrection is the power of seership.</u>"

In the Bible, it reads: "<u>For the testimony of Jesus is the spirit of prophecy.</u>" (Rev. 19:10).

That passage refers to the resurrection of the dormant glands of the sixth and seventh sense powers of man, and the evidence of their resurrection or activation is the power of seership, that strange power of the senses which raises man from the common five to the rare seven sense plane of consciousness.

The Apocalypse treats quite fully of the spiritual and psychic forces in man, but nowhere gives even a clue to the process by which these forces can be resurrected or activated. That was the top secret of the Masters and was never committed to writing.

The most remarkable feature of the Bible is the skillfull manner in which the scheming church fathers wove facts and falsehoods together.

We defy any one to read one chapter or one paragraph in the Bible and find in it either truth or falsehood separatedly stated. Each falsehood is so inseparably connected with an undeniable truth, and the true and the false are so intricately and delicately interwove, that it is absolutely impossible for the unprepared mind to separate the one from the other.

The Bible has gone out to the world and has chained in darkness and ignorance more people than any other secular book has ever done, exactly as it was planned by the cunning church fathers.

These deceived people must live in that darkness until they evolve to such mental ability that they can winnow the true from the false in this book a nd come to understand its fradulent character.

The distortions in the Bible are so numerous and so cleverly made that they can be detected only by an expert in the Ancient Arcane Science.

The Masters who developed this science knew that the creative or trans-formative Intelligence is a phenomenon that rises from the orderly operation of polarized atoms, and this polarization they represented in the Caduceus by a white (positive) and a black (negative) serpent, also called the Good and Bad Serpent.

Cosmic Intelligence of the atom attains its highest point in man, making him the Supreme Being of all organized bodies in both the visible and the invisible worlds.

The anthropomorphic god of theology is an imaginary entity invented by the church and in which they centered and combined all the powers and principles manifested in the lawful processes of polarized atoms, plus solar radiation, the animating principle.

Man can never rise above his present low level and emerge from the fog of illusion until he is made to realize that he is the Lord of the whole earth and the God of the Universe (Zech. 4:14).

DEATH

The words "die" and "death" in the philosophy of the Ancient Masters did not imply extinction. They used these terms to designate Renovation, Re-Birth.

For the Life Power in man is the same as that which constantly renews vitality in all the realms of Nature, as explained in the Bible.

That which thou sowest is not quickened, except it die (1 Chor. 15:36).

Then the dying process is illustrated in the planting of grain. The grain does not die. The physical form disintegrates and returns to dust, as the Life Principle in it lives on again in the new plant.

One Life; Eternal Life animates all living things, as stated under Solar Radiation.

Recent discoveries that physical matter is condensed spiritual substance have shocked material science.

We can now comprehend somewhat the teachings of the Masters that the invisible things are clearly understood by their visible manifestation (Rom. 1:20) and that Birth and Death are names applied to the Visible changes occurring constantly in the Cosmic Cycle.

We must not be led astray by what we see. Appearances are illusions. We reason from what we think we see and say that man dies, or that the Sun rises. Man only appears to die, as the Sun only appears to rise.

The Bible says "We shall not sleep (in death), but we shall all be changed (to spiritual immortality). And so death is swallowed up in victory."

The immortality of Life was common knowledge with the Ancient Masters and will be again when the false teachings of the church have been exploded by proper education of the masses.

"As we have (all) borne the image of the earthy, we shall (all) also bear

(Note: This page was typed on a different typewriter than the other pages. However, the complete text is intact and has not been altered.)

the image of the heavenly." (1 Cor. 15:49).

This declaration is not conditioned on any belief. It includes all men, regardless of their belief. (Mk. 16:16).

That Mythical Jesus

The gospel narrative of the biblical Jesus is largely an allegorical story of the Soul but distorted and literalized to make it appear as the story of a man.

The story was brought to Asia Minor from India by that great teacher of the first century, previously mentioned.

The story alluded to the life of Krishna, who symbolized the Sun. The Hindus called the Sun "Kris."

The four stages of earthly being, infancy, youth, maturity, and death, are represented in Nature by the four seasons of the zodiacal year; thus the astronomical significance of the allegory.

The allegory was dramatized in the Ancient Mysteries to teach the neophyte the path of Life.

The parallel of man's earthy life was represented as the Fall of Spirit from the celestial realm of Light into the terrestrial realm of Darkness, in which the Celestial Body is imprisoned in its physical envelope (1 Cor. 15:40); its defilement therein by desire and lust and its purification in physical death and its return to its celestial home.

This dramatized allegory was distorted and literalized in the New Testament to change the life of Krishna, symbol of the Sun, to that of Jesus as a man, which, joined with the original Hindu fable of Krishna, became the fabulous Life of the gospel Christ, Christos, Kristos.

Ancient Initiation

Dr. Angus wrote: "Initiation proper into the Ancient Mysteries was considered a physical death from which the Initiate rose through rebirth (born again). The hour of midnight was often chosen as the appropriate time for initiation. There was a familiar word-play on the words "initiation" and "dying." "To die is to be initiated," said Plato.

In the ceremonies of Initiation, the neophyte was shown the mummied form of Asarus (Osiris, and called Lazarus in the Bible--Jn. 11), lying on its funeral bier, and to him the Hierophant said:

"Cast thine eyes upon this motionless figure; after death thou wilt resemble it."

When the neophyte was "resurrected" from symbolical death, as practiced

-18-

in the third degree of modern Masonry, he knew by that experience the great secret of initiation, and what occurs in physical death. He learned by actual experience that Life is eternal and did not have to rely for the information on the empty jargon of a preacher.

In the oldest of all Bibles, the Egyptian Book of the Dead, the Spirit, in the form of a Dove with outstretched wings, hovers over the body and is made to say to the candidate:

"I have the power to be born a second time (Jn. 3:3). As Spirit I enter the body and come forth again as Spirit and look down upon my physical form, which is that called man.

That is incarnation and was taught by the Masters as the burial of Spirit in Matter. They called it a living death--a state that carries life on but under conditions dramatized as Death in the Ancient Mysteries.

Cicero said that the Initiates not only receive lessons which made life more agreeable, but drew from the ceremonies happy hopes for the future life.

Socrates said that those admitted to the Mysteries possessed, when dying, the most glorious hopes for eternity.

Pindar wrote: "Happy is he who has passed through the Mysteries. He knows the origin and the end of (terrestial) life."

In the finale, initiation in the Ancient Mysteries was the presentation of knowledge of the remarkable CHANGE that occurs at death.

Paul shouted: "Behold, I show you a mystery: We shall not sleep (in death), but we shall all be changed" (to spiritual immortality) (1 Cor. 15:51).

Death is the natural, final rite that releases Spiritual Man from his physical prison. The Ancient Masters said:

"The Real Man is never born, nor does he die. Unborn, undying ancient, perpetual, and eternal, he has endured and will endure forever. The body dissolves and returns to dust, but He who hath occupied it remaineth unharmed and unchanged."

The Future Life

The Ancient Masters taught that what we call death is a state of transition wherein man's spiritual consciousness rules supreme because it is released from the limitations imposed by the physical organism. Man is then able to see both sides of his dual nature and to sense his spiritual self as the Real Man and his physical self as the shadow man.

At transition (physical death), the substance of the visible body falls entirely out of the range of the Great Cosmic Circuit of Life, and, under the law governing inert matter, it disintegrates into gases and fluids. But the subconscious Mind (Spiritual Man) remains intact, unaltered, unharmed by that mysterious change.

In the unconscious state, man's conscious Mind is blank and inactive. Suspended are the faculties of seeing, hearing, smelling, tasting, and feeling. If we open the eye of a dead man, he cannot see anything. The senses of the physical plane are then incompetent to register impressions conveying any intelligence.

The Supreme Universal Consciousness maintains its perpetually active state so that the physiological processes of the unconscious body continue uninterruptedly. In fact, the S. U. C. is so alert that if the unconscious body is removed from a comfortable to a chilly room, the body termperature automatically changes to meet the hostile conditions of the colder environment.

In like manner other disturbances are met. If the arms or legs of the unconscious body are artificially exercised, the physiological processes quicken to supply the additional energy required. That illustrates the power of the Subconscious Mind to protect the unconscious body, despite the fact that the unconscious body is unaware of it.

This unconscious state is only temporary. At transition (physical death), a similar condition occurs but remains permanent.

Transition (physical death) is the end of physical consciousness and the Subconscious Power rules supreme, being no longer bound and limited by the physical consciousness.

Modern science studies the physical side of man only and sees nothing but his visible form, which it mistakes for the Real Man. In the end, it is left empty-handed, for the physical man is only the shadow man.

There is one striking feature of the reports of those who have been on the border-line of transition but did not pass over (Ps. 104:9). These reports all agree.

The little girl was just able to talk, and she described in a childish way what she experienced in her unconscious state. She had never heard the things she related, yet her report was identical with all the others. What did they report?

The secret of what occurs in man's mind at the moment of transition and later was taught in the Egyptian Mysteries.

The rites of these ancient dramas, "commencing in gloom and sorrow, and ending in light and joy, dimly shadowed forth the strange passage of man from physical mortality to spiritual immortality."

Traces of these things appear in the Bible, but only occult students understand.

"I will ransom them from the power of the grave" (Hos. 13:14). "In the twinkling of an eye, the dead shall be raised incorruptible and we shall be changed. For this corruptible must put on incorruption, and this mortal must put on immortality" (1. Cor. 15:52, 53).

These dark passages appear in clear light when we know the esoteric meaning.

A certain man lay dying. A man noted for the trusting curiosity of his mind. He was a Free-thinker. Many were the nights he had sat thrashing our with his friends the great question--What comes after death?

Now, in dying, he was only seconds away from the answer. Suddenly, his eyes opened. They seemed to penetrate thru the ceiling and beyond.

A happy smile lit his face. As the last breath left his body--"Ah! " he whispered..."The Great Secret at last! "

What was the Great Secret he saw unfold as he slipped out of this life?

This is the story told by those who have been on the borderline of transition, but did not pass over:

There is at first a sense of surprising levity of the body. That appears as the first factor which impresses the subconscious mind of the unconscious man.

Long before the unconscious man is willing to let nurse or doctor know that strange things are happening, he begins to sense that he is not lying so heavily.

At first he thinks it is the imagination. Then he begins to sense a pleasant warmth, and to feel that he could rise from the bed and nothing could s top him.

The room that was only a few feet distant begins to appear farther away. It is not due to fading eyesight, as he still recognizes those present.

It is the secret of the Fourth Dimension. Man begins to sense himself in a world devoid of both space and time, which means existence in the Fourth Dimension. But none of the persons mentioned, except the philosopher, had ever heard of the Fourth Dimension.

Then the voices of the persons present begin to grow dim until it seems as if they were at the very end of the hall. This is a great moment for the unconscious person, for it indicates a fading out of physical impressions.

Eventually, the unconscious man could see nothing but his body on the bed. Not with his physical eyes, but with his spiritual sight. He seemed to be several feet above his body, gazing down at it.

Between him and his body appeared a dim haze. The philosopher described it as the aura. Another said it looked like the Silver Cord mentioned in the Bible (Eccl. 12:6). Still another described it as being similar to the umbilical cord but not so solid.

The fact is, they all saw something between them and their body, as they could feel the separation slowly taking place.

Another feature is, they had no desire to return to their body or to stop the separating process. But they did have a feeling of deep sorrow for those weeping around the body.

They sense that sorrow and feel they must return to relieve it. But as for themselves, the sense of levity, of great freedom from all pain and suffering, the thrill of the new existence, give them an impelling urge to let the changing process continue and become permanent.

All accounts agree that there seems to be a dual power present: One trying to hold them in the body and the other trying to draw them awa; and in that perplexing state, some of them waver.

Finally, as to those who go through the experience and return, they are drawn back into their body. They feel themselves cramped, shut in, and crushed; and at once their physical sensations begin to return.

They begin to feel uncomfortably warm instead of the pleasant cooling sensation. They begin to feel heavy and weighted down, as if there were a weight on their chest. It is difficult to breathe. Their eyelids are hard to open, but they slowly do--and that is the first sign that they are returning to consciousness.

Sometimes it may be several days before they are able to talk. But they know all that is occurring around them.

That is the strange story of the border-line state. The stories not only all agree, but they relate the same understandable events.

Such are the secrets of the Future Life, discovered by the Ancient Masters and taught to their disciples.

Astral Projection

We shall notice some more border-line cases. In 1936, Juliette Neel, of Texas, underwent an operation. When she inhaled the ether to make her unconscious, she says a strange thing happened, which she thus describes:

"I heard the doctor talking in low tones as he ordered instruments, and suddenly I was no longer conscious of being in my body. I seemed to be above my body looking down on the operation.

"I saw the doctor insert instruments into my body. Then I spoke and said, "I know what you are doing to my body."

"The doctor and nurses were startled and did not move for a moment. I went on describing the operation and trying to prove that I was conscious of everything and was not in the body.

"When the operation was over, I returned to my body. There was an interval of unconsciousness, and when I awoke, I found the doctor and nurses were amused by my description of the operation told to them while under the effect of the ether." (Condensed from Fate Magazine, Oct. 1957).

Margaret Linden, writing in Fate Magazine, said:

"I am certain that Life continues after (physical) death, because I was once permitted to cross the threshold between them."

She became ill and was rushed to a hospital for an operation. About two hours after the operation, she says:

"I was back in bed and was reviving from the effect of the anaesthetic and heard myself cry despairingly, over and over, "Don't send me back!"

She continues:

"I can further remember trying frantically to move my inert body and being restrained by the doctor who held both my hands.

"He was speaking quietly, insistently, striving to impress on my subconscious mind that it must hold fast to the remembrance of why I was begging not to be 'sent back.'

"The next day when I returned to full consciousness, the doctor was there and asked me, 'Did I remember?' I did, and do now.

"At some time during the operation, I--my spirit--left my body. I remember that I was flying and knew this was no dream. For I had died. I knew it, and I welcomed it.

"It was far more wonderful than any dream. I was no longer imprisoned in my body. I was free and lighter than thought. I had no weight, no substance at all. I knew that I was no longer a (physical) person.

"I was just an essence, a vital spark, equipped with thoughts, feelings, and senses. The feeling above all else was that of extraordinary happiness.

"I could hear sweet music, and it seemed that I was the center of it."

"As I was savoring this ecstasy in its entirety, a voice in me commanded: 'You must go back; you must go back.'

"I felt as if I were being pushed downward, and I cried, I implored, but again came the command: 'You must go back.'"

"Down I came, faster and faster, until, with a crash, I felt myself being pushed into what seemed to be a coffin of lead, which my spirit knew was my body.

"After I told this to the doctor, he informed me that toward the end of the operation, I had no pulse, no heart beat, no breath. I was apparently dead. He had immediately inserted his fingers through the incision in my body and was able to massage my heart, hoping to start its action.

"He succeeded—and I am alive again" (Condensed from Fate Magazine).

Life in the physical body is wonderful; and how grand is transition.

The levity of the body, the freedom of all restraints, the absence of time and darkness and of all disagreeable sensations.

This knowledge lifts the veil and reveals the arcane science of the Ancient Masters.

By conducting the candidate to the very border-line state in the initiation, "the abode of (physical) death," he was taught that when man dies physically, the Living Spiritual Man is withdrawn from the material counterpat under spiritual conditions in that "New Life beyond the grave, which is everlasting."

PRE-EXISTENCE

OF

MAN

By

Prof. Hilton Hotema

In Two Parts

Part II

THE BIBLE SAYS
Behold, a Door opened in Heaven (Rev. 4:1).

Or ever the Silver Cord be loosed, or the Golden Bowl be broken (Eccl. 12:6).

And Jakob dreamed, and behold a ladder set up on the earth, and the top of it reached to heaven; and the angels of God (were) ascending and descending on it (Gen. 28:12).

In this work we interpret this mysterious symbology, show that it is all intimately related and represents certain psycho-bio-physio-logical processes of the earthly Temple of God in which the Spirit of God dwells (1 Cor. 3:16). But our interpretation, based on the Ancient Wisdom, is far different from any that the Christians ever heard.

Chapter No. 20

Mysteries in the Universe

In his work *Morals and Dogma of Freemasonry* (indexed cloth), Albert Pike discussed some of the mysteries in the Universe that are ever taking place around us; so trite and common to us that we never notice nor reflect upon them. We can do no better to impress these mysteries upon the reader than to repeat some of Pike's statements.

Wise men tell us, he says, of the laws that regulate the motions of the spheres, which, flashing in huge circles and spinning on their axes, are also ever darting with great speed thru the infinities of Space.

They tell us learnedly of centripetal and centrifugal forces, repulsion and attraction, and all the other high-sounding terms invented to hide a want of meaning.

Here are two small seeds, much alike in appearance, and two larger ones. We hand them to the learned scientist who tells us how combustion goes on in the lungs and how plants are fed with phosphorus and carbon and the alkalies and silex. Let him decompose them, analyze them, torture them in all the ways he knows. The net result of each is a little sugar, a little fibrin, a little water-carbon, potassium, sodium, and the like.

We plant them in the ground; the rains mosten them, the sun shines on them, and slender shoots spring up and grow--and what a miracle is the mere growth,--the force, the capacity by which the feeble shoots, which a little worm can nip off with a single snap of its mandibles, attracts from the earth, the air, and the moisture the different elements, so learned cataloged by science, with which the plant increases in stature and rises toward the sky.

One plant grows to a slender, fragile, feeble stalk, soft of texture, just an ordinary weed; another a strong bush, of woody fiber, armed with thorns and sturdy enough to defy the winds; the third a tender tree, subject to damage by frost and looked down upon by all the forest; while another spreads its rugged arms abroad and cares for neither frost nor ice, nor the snows that lie around its roots for months.

Out of the brown earth the colorless invisible air, the limpid rain-water, and the sunlight, the chemical powers of the seeds have extracted various shades of green that paint the leaves which put forth in the spring upon the plants, the shrubs, and the trees.

Later on come the flowers, the vivid colors of the rose, the brilliance of the carnation, the modest blush of the apple bloom, and the snow white of the orange.

Whence come the colors of the leaves and the flowers? By what process of chemistry are they extracted from the carbon, the phosphorus, the lime, the water, the air, and the sunlight? Is it any greater miracle to make the visible out of the invisible? Here is an illustration of its being done.

Inhale the delicious perfumes of the flowers. Whence have they come? By what combination of acids and alkalies could the chemist's laboratory produce them?

27

And on two there comes the fruit--the ruddy apple and the golden orange.

Pluck them, open them. How totally different the texture and fabric. The flavor, how entirely dissimilar; the perfume of each distinct from its flower and from the other.

Whence the flavor and this new perfume? The same earth, air, water, and light have been made to furnish a different flavor to each fruit, a different perfume to each fruit not only, but to each flower.

Is it any more of a problem whence come thought and will and perception and all the phenomena of mind, than this, whence come the colors, the perfumes, the flavor of the fruit and the flower?

And in each fruit it seeds, each gifted with the same wondrous power of reproduction--each with the same wondrous forces concealed in it, to be again in turn evolved. Forces that lived three thousand years in the grain of wheat found in the wrappings of an Egyptian mummy; forces of which learning, science, and wisdom know no more than they do of the nature and laws of Creation.

What can we know of the nature, and how can we understand the powers and mode of operation of the Solar Man when the glossy leaves, the golden flower, and the ruddy fruit of the trees are miracles entirely beyond our comprehension?

We but hide our ignorance in a cloud of words, and the words too often are mere combinations of sounds without any meaning.

Who has yet made us to understand, with all his learned words, how the image of an external object comes to and fixes itself upon the retina of the eye; and when there, how that mere empty, unsubstantial image becomes transmuted into the wondrous phenomenon we call sight?

Or how the waves of the air striking upon the tympanum of the ear--those thin, invisible waves--produce the equally wondrous phenomenon of hearing and become the roar of the tornado, the crash of the thunder, the voice of the ocean, the chirping of the cricket, the sweet notes of the mocking-bird, or the magic melody of the violin of Paganini?

At this point Pike could well have added that we know nothing about how solar electricity, flowing into the brain thru the Silver Cord which we shall notice later, produces the strange phenomenon termed Life, whose work in the brain exhibits the mind of the master, the intelligence of the professor, the consciousness of the doctor, or the logic of the lawyer.

Or how the mind rises superior to the Time-Space element, as in dreams, and takes us back in a moment for more than half a century in our life to the days when we were young and were fighting with our comrades in the Philippine insurrection in 1899, 1900, and 1901.

Or how the clairvoyant rises to the fourth dimensional mind and is able to see the past life of a certain individual, or how the hypnotist can send his subject back thru the days of his life to the point of antecedent incarnations, as Morey Bernstein did in the case of Bridey Murphy.

Our senses are mysteries to science, and we are mysteries to ourselves. Science has taught us nothing but words as to the nature of our sensations,

28

our perceptions, our cognizances, the origin of our thoughts and ideas.

The great Carrel declared that man diffuses thru space and that the psychological frontiers of the individual in space and time are obviously suppositions and not actualities (*Man The Unknown*, p. 259).

What does science know of Substance? Men even doubt whether it exists. Philosophers tell us that our senses make known to us only the attributes of substance, extension, expansion, hardness, color, and the like; but not the thing itself that is extended, solid, black, or white.

What a wondrous mystery there is in heat and light, existing we know not how, with certain limits, narrow in comparison with infinity, beyond which, on every side, stretch out infinite space and blackness of unimaginable darkness, and the intensity of the inconceivable cold.

And what a mystery are the effects of heat and cold upon the fluid we call water. What a mystery lies hidden in the snowflake and in every crystal of ice and in their transformation into invisible vapor that rises from the ocean and the land and floats away above the summits of the mountain tops.

Think what would happen if the law of attraction, or affinity, or cohesion for example, failed to function. The whole material world, with its solid granite and adamant, its veins of gold and silver, its trap and porphyry, its huge coal beds, our own frames, and the very rocks of this apparently indestructible earth, would instantaneously dissolve with all suns and stars and planets throughout all the Universe into a thin, invisible vapor of infinitely small particles or atoms, diffused thru infinite space; and with them light and heat would disappear.

How can we, with our limited mental vision, expect to grasp and comprehend them?

Infinite Space, stretching out from us every way, without limit; infinite Time, without beginning or end; and We, here and now, in the center of each.

An infinity of suns, the nearest of which only diminish in size, viewed with the most powerful telescope; each with its retinue of worlds; infinite numbers of such suns, so remote from us that their light would not reach us, journeying thru an infinity of time, while the light that has reached us, from some that we seem to see, has been upon its journey for fifty centuries.

Our world spinning upon its axis and rushing ever in its circuit round the sun; and the sun and all our system, revolving round some great central point; and that, with suns, stars, and worlds evermore flashing onward with incredible speed thru illimitable space.

And then, in every drop of water that we drink, in every morsel of much of our food, in the air, in the earth, in the sea, incredible multitudes of living creatures, invisible to the naked eye, of a smallness beyond belief, yet organized, living, feeding, perhaps with consciousness of identity and memory and intelligence.

Such are some of the mysteries of the great Universe. And yet we, whose life and that of the world on which we live, from but a point in the center of

29

infinite Time; we who support animaculae within, and on whom vegetables grow
without, would fain learn the secrets of this Universe and of ourselves.
--Excerpted from pp. 526-530.

****

Chapter No. 21

MANY BODIES

Various authors write about the Astral Body, the Ethereal Body, the Solar
Body, etc.

Paracelsus said: "Man is a Sun and a Moon and a Heaven filled with Stars.
The world is a Man, and the light of the Sun and the Stars is in his body.
The Ethereal Body cannot be grasped, and yet it is substance."

Dr. M. Doreal wrote: "The physical body is built upon the Astral Body as
a foundation." (Astral Plane, p.8).

In "The Perfect Way," A.B. Kingsford said: "The Soul is a Spiritual Sun,
corresponding in all things with the Solar Orb . . . The Soul's history is one,
and this is a history corresponding with the Sun's."

Another author stated: "The immortal Augoedies, or Solar Body, is of
atomic, non-molecular substance."

Elizabeth Towne observed: "There is a real Sun Center in us, the Solar
Plexus . . . The Solar Plexus is the point where life is born--where the
Uncreate becomes Create; the unorganized becomes organized; the unconscious
becomes conscious; the invisible becomes visible, the immeasurable becomes
measurable." (The Solar Plexus, 1907, pp. 6, 7).

Did these writers know they were discussing the same Body? We shall
strive to harmonize their statements, dispel the fog of confusion, and lead to
the Light the man in darkness.

CREATION

As we use the term Creation, we refer not to an event that occurred
thousands or millions of years ago, but to the events taking place daily right
under our nose.

We see babies born and men die, yet most of us fail to realize that we
are witnessing the eternal processes of creation in action.

The Ancient Masters saw creative work as a constant and eternal process,
always in action, without beginning and without end. They illustrated the
process by the use of a dot, in which is contained potentially all that later
appears actually, and showed that the dot may be expanded as a circle to
infinity and extended as a line to infinity.

The Masters postulated that each material form has an immaterial counterpart or pattern that had no beginning and no end--the postulate of Archetypes
or Telarche.

30

In the case of man, that immaterial form is the invisible astral body, or ethereal body, or solar body—the Solar Spark, the immortal Augoeides, the Greek Soma Heliakon, and is constituted of atomic, non-molecular substance.

In the creative process, the invisible Solar Spark expands and extends, unfolds and develops and builds physical man, who appears clad in the garment of the Cosmos, corresponding in color, number, and vibration to the Solar System as it was at the moment of conception, at the moment of the beginning of the expansion and extension process of the invisible Solar Spark.

THE ATOM

Science has somewhat discovered the atom. Everything is atomic, and we are entering the age of atomism.

The solar system is a cosmic atom. Each planet is an atom. Solar Man is an Atomic Unit.

Infinite Intelligence thrills thru every atom; and every atom has the potentiality of self-consciousness.

The Ego, the Nous, the Pre-Existing Man, the Potential Man, appears in the visible world in four bodies, constituted of Four Seed Atoms. And atoms are so small that 900,000 of them could rest side by side on a pin point (*Cosmic Creation*, p. 3).

Molecules are composed of atoms, and molecules are so small that they are too tiny to reflect visible light, hence they must forever be invisible to us.

If the molecules of a thimbleful of water were each magnified to the size of an average orange, they would cover the entire United States with a layer of oranges 1,000 feet deep.

And the 100 or more atoms in each of these tiny molecules are globular systems in which electrons revolve with great speed around their common center of attraction, like the planets and the sun of our solar system.

The development of man's four bodies is the work of these Four Seed Atoms

Regardless of the size of the physical body, the Ego remains the same directing, governing principle. If his physical body grew as big as a mountain, man could not exhibit any more or any other qualities than those he has when he is only that invisible Solar Spark.

The size of the physical body has no effect on the Ego, and the size of that body is due to the accumulation of more atoms under the law of polarity.

As we shall later explain, at the death of the physical body, these accumulated atoms return to the cosmic reservoir as the body disintegrates; but the Four Seed Atoms, the Ego, remain stable and intact as a Cosmic Unit.

An atom is a miniature solar system, with "planets" (electrons) revolving within the infinitesimal space of the atom, around a common center of attraction, at a terrific speed of from 10,000 to 90,000 miles a second. That force of the atoms is the force of the body.

31

The chemical atom is so small that it requires a group of not less than a billion to form a speck that is barely visible under the most powerful microscope; and a thousand of such groups would have to be united to make a speck just visible to the naked eye.

And that is a description of Solar Man. That is the Point of Creation. In that Point are the various bodies mentioned by writers as Astral, Ethereal, Solarical, etc.

ATOMIC PROCESSES

It is difficult for scientists to believe that the atom possesses conscious intelligence, know its work, and does its work perfectly when not hindered by any interference, such, for instance, as the work of a medical doctor trying to change or control the body's function by the administration of various poisons erroneously called medicine.

The great Carrel declared that "The existence of (the) Intelligence (of the atom) is a primary datum of observation" (*Man The Unknown*, p. 121).

Carrel showed how this Atomic Intelligence appears in the work of the body cells and declared that the cells have an inherent knowledge, a prevision, of the structure they are to build, and—

"From substance contained in the (gases of the) blood plasma, they synthetize the building material and even the builders" (p. 108). He continued:

"The cells seem to remember their original unity, even when they become the elements of an innumerable multitude. They know spontaneously the functions attributed to them in the organized whole (body).

"If we cultivate epithelial cells over a period of time, quite apart from the animal to which they belong, they (automatically) arrange themselves in a mossic, exactly as if to protected is lacking.

"Isolated cells possess the singular power of reproducing, without apparent direction or purpose, the edifices characterizing each organ (of the body).

"If a few red corpuscles, impelled by gravity, flow from a drop of blood placed in liquid plasma and form a tiny stream, banks are soon built up. Then these banks cover themselves with filaments of fibrin, forming a pipe, thru which the red cells flow just as in a blood vessel. Next, leucocytes come, adhere to the inner wall of the pipe, and cover it with their undulating membrane.

(Note: This is the mucous membrane that lines all tubes and internal cavities in the body. Hotema).

"The bloodstream now assumes the form of a capillary (blood) vessel, enveloped in a layer of contractile cells.

"And thus, the isolated red and white corpuscles (of the blood) constuct a segment of circulatory apparatus, although there is neither heart, circulation, nor tissue to be irrigated." (p. 107).

The Intelligence which directs and performs this magic work is the

32

Creative Principle inherent in the atom, and called "God" by the enslaved multitude that supports the very institution by which the multitude is enslaved.

The Creative Power, the Creative Intelligence, the Intelligence of the Universe, and of Man, are inherent in the Atom. The experiments of science prove this, and yet the scientists deny the existence of what they see.

Matter is composed of chemical atoms, and they exhibit a definite degree of Intelligence.

For instance, liver cells know their kind of work, and so do all the cells, organs, and tissues of the body.

The Cosmic Intelligence in the atoms uses the cells as instruments to do the work they are intended to do.

The eye of the body cannot see. Cosmic Intelligence uses the eye as an instrument for the purpose of seeing.

The optic nerve receives vibrations that are transmitted by the nerve to the sight center of the brain, and there Mind translates the vibrations into sight. The same is true of hearing, smelling, tasting, and feeling.

The Intelligence of the cells, of all parts of the body, including the Mind, is the Intelligence of the Atom.

This Intelligence appears as a subconscious power in the body and enables the body to perceive the present and future needs of the body and to act accordingly.

TIME-SPACE

The significance of the Time-Space element is not the same for the cells and atoms of the body, nor for the Subconscious Department of the Mind, as it is for the Conscious Department of Mind, limited by five faulty senses.

The work of the body and its cells shows that the Subconscious perceives the remote as well as the near, the future as well as the present. The teleological correlation of organic processes is evident.

Body functions reveal the existence of the power of Prevision and Provision, by virtue of which the body may rise superior to heredity, as well as to environment, until it meets and masters the conditions of a progressive or an established achievement.

Prevision is the power to visualize and realize the ultimate effect of any harmful habit or substance and guard against it by vigorous reaction, yielding to its inimical influence thru the Law of Adjustment only when the primary reaction is disregarded.

At this point we have before us the entire field of good health and bad health and the entire field of "medical practice."

As the body struggles against the effects of the harmful habits and harmful substances which enter it, and are forced into it, painful symptoms appear.

33

The doctor is trained to group these symptoms together, give them names (diagnosis), and term them "diseases" that may kill the patient if not treated and "cured" by the administration of poisons falsely called medicine.

No doubt medical art is ignorant of the way the "immunizing poisons" affect the body. They weaken the vital body by dulling the nerves. That weakened, decreased vitality makes the body unable to react "acutely" to the damaging internal poisons.

The "immunized" body is now too weak to throw off these poisons in the reaction called "acute disease," and so the "acute disease" has been conquered, and medical science has won another victory in the "war on disease."

But what are the actual facts? These poisons now remain in the "immunized" and weakened body, corrode the internal organs, and in due time develop into dangerous chronic disorders that "baffle medical science."

The ultimate result is that instead of Johnny's having measles, mumps, or chicken-pox at the age of six or seven, and thus eliminating the damaging internal poisons, they remain in the body and he dies of cancer or diabetes when he is 35 or 40.

Medical art admits that chronic disorders are on the increase but claims it is because people are living longer. That is another medical falsehood and another exhibition of medical ignorance.

Provision is the power of selective adaptation, which is operative in both the Conscious and Subconscious departments of the body.

Adaptation involves selection, and the power of selection places the body on the plane of Mind. The ultimate act of Mind is the appropriation or rejection of the present materials of supply, which acts imply the qualities of intelligence, sensation, and volition.

The living organism is self-conserving in the highest degree. There is reason and purpose in all of its structures and functions; and these are designed to accomplish specific results and definite ends.

The true scientist opines that organized bodies exist as such by virtue of a final cause; that purpose alone rules supreme as the law governing all organized nature; and that in organized bodies nothing is in vain.

Not to know the purpose of the law does not subvert the facts, nor make necessary or legitimate any procedure contrary to the facts—such as giving poisons, called medicine, to the sick that would never be given to the well, under the absurd theory that these poisons are beneficial to the sick but are detrimental to the well.

CREATIVE WORK

In "The Mysterious Sphinx" we showed that this strange creature was a symbol of the Masters which represented the Four Cosmic Elements of Creation, Fire, Air, Water, and Earth; while in our work titled "The Magic Wand" we explained that the White and Black Serpents entwined around the Staff of the Caduceus represented the Positive and Negative Principles of Creative Processes.

Conscious Intelligence in the Atom rises to its highest point on the material plane in Man, making him, as stated in the Bible, the Supreme Being of all organized forms in both the visible and invisible worlds (Gen. 1:26).

Creative processes are ruled and directed by the Law of Polarity, and the power of polarity inheres in the Atom. Without Polarity there would be no Universe.

Creative Intelligence appears as a principle that rises before our mind in the fixed and orderly processes of Polarized Atoms.

Where does the church God come into the picture? Man created him and put him on the Throne, and then this God created everything.

That God is a figment of the imagination, in which are combined all the elements, powers and principles of Polarized Atoms that doeth the work.

That imaginary God was born of the impressions made upon the Mind of Man by his observation of the mysterious work performed by these atomic powers and principles, and which he blindly believed to be the mystic work of an anthropomorphic God. Of course, that statement applies to the masses and not to the Masters.

The Creator is not an objective reality as taught by the church, but a combination of Cosmic Principles inherent in the atom and pervading all things.

Man is an infinitely compounded Unit, a living mirror of the Universe. He is the embodiment of all the powers and principles of the Universe, all of which are summarized, recapitulized and perfectionized in Man.

Man knows little about himself, even his physical self, much less of his Solarical Self.

The actual facts are so contrary to the theories of evolution, and to the speculations and assumptions of science, that men of science dismiss the subject with a shrug and a sneer, and cover up their ignorance by asserting there is nothing to it,--just "heathenish superstition."

There is no Organized Entity in the Universe that is higher than Man. He is the Supreme Being of the Organic World.

- -

Chapter No. 22

Man, The Unknown

In our work titled "Mystery of Man," we have shown that we know so little about the true nature of man, many of the statements in the ancient scriptures which actually refer to man, his constitution and the functions of his body, go over the head and cannot be understood by us.

Consider the great discoveries that have come in rapid succession in recent years.

Consider how the limits of our little world are extending and expanding at an accelerating speed, especially on the super-physical side by means of these discoveries, which are now unfolding a hitherto hidden vista of facts, within the ambit of wireless-transmission, television, stereoscopic cinematic sound and color projection, electric wave length, radar, infra-red, violet, x-ray, and other rays, and now atomic power.

The Invisible World

All of these falling into place as electro-mechanical projections of television, premonition, divination, intuition, telepathy, clairvoyance, clairaudience, prevoyance, and the transmutation of elements by the alchemists. And these advances now moving into the "occult" or metaphysical field, are rapidly leading us toward the border zone of what is termed fourth dimensional space or the invisible world.

But in spite of all this progress, the intensive study that scientists have made of man in the last two centuries, has increased the confusion by adding to the mystery instead of solving it.

One of the greatest of these, Dr. Alexis Carrel, concluded 33 years of brilliant biological research at the Rockefeller Institute in 1939, and wrote a valuable book of 346 pages, published in 1935, which he titled "Man, The Unknown," in his effort to summarize in a few words the conclusion he had reached concerning man as a result of his long years of labor. On page four he said:

"In fact, our ignorance (of man) is profound. Most of the questions put to themselves by those who study human beings remain without answer. Immense regions of our inner world (of man's body) are still unknown."

The tone of this frank admission sounds quite different from the boasting propaganda issued by the medical world about the conquest of disease, the immunization of the body against disease, and similar statements that are nothing more than a drama of words used to conceal ignorance and mislead the masses.

A Physical Vehicle

What is the body? It is the common error of modern science to identify the physical body with man, whereas the body is simply a vehicle for expression on the physical plane, and is discarded when no longer needed.

The Bible mentions bodies as celestial and terrestrial. Paul said there is a natural body and a spiritual (celestial) body (1 Cor. 15:44).

The natural body is simply a vehicle of manifestation, appropriate to the conditions and the environment in which our lives are cast.

Men, beasts, fishes and birds all have bodies specifically designed to fit them in their environment, and to function adequately in the element in which they are produced and placed.

The body is not identical with the force which animates it. The body is the instrument only.

What Is Death

We must realize that death means only the dissolution and disintegration of the physical vehicle.

When Paul said "the last enemy to be destroyed is death" (1 Cor. 15:26), he meant that man must drive from his mind the false impression that death is the end of life.

According to the Bible, man lives to die and dies to live. That is what the biblical scribe meant when he wrote: Except a man be born again (in the process called death), he cannot see the invisible Kingdom of Life (Jn. 3:3,5,7).

The same thought was expressed in these words: For our light affliction (death), which is but for a moment, worketh for us a far more exceeding and eternal weight of glory (immortality) (2 Cor. 4:17).

What would you say if you could see man leaving his body in the process called death?

You do not understand that dying is a physiological process which is governed by cosmic law just as truly as is the process of birth.

You do not realize that the process of dying is not the end of man, but the end of his body only.

Job made a mistake when he said, "If a man die, shall he live again" (14:14).

Other ancient scribes voiced the truth when they wrote: "Your heart (Soul) shall live forever. I shall not die, but live. We shall not die" (Ps. 22:26; 118:17; Hab. 1:12).

Man longs for eternal life. He has spent billions of dollars to cover the earth with synagogs, temples and churches in which he seeks to learn the Secret of Life; but his teachers fail him.

In these halls of worship, man has had millions of sermons shouted at him to have faith. He has read books on why he should have faith. They all tried to argue him into a belief of Immortality.

But not a priest, nor a preacher, nor an author seemed to know enough about the Secret of Life to cite any law to support their arguments.

If Immortality is a fact, it is governed by cosmic law. For every condition, every action, every cause, every effect,--all are ruled by fixed and unchanging laws.

The Bible says: "Behold, I show you a mystery; we shall not sleep (in death), but we shall all be CHANGED (to Immortality) in a moment, in the twinkling of an eye" (1 Cor. 15:51, 52).

That statement is true; it is scientific; for it is based on a definite law; and that law is the Cosmic Cycle.

This biblical "mystery" is solved by a discovery of the law.

Symbol of Creation

The great things of the universe are always simple; too simple to be

37

noticed. The great truths of the world are always simple.

The complexity and confusion met with in the world are always found in the realm of fraud and deceit, such as modern theology and medical art.

The ancient symbol of Creation was as simple as the Kingdom of God described by the gospel Jesus (Mat. 13:31). Just a Dot in a Circle.

The symbol did not represent a garden, with pearly gates and golden streets, with a castle in the center, and a king sitting on a golden throne. It represented a simple Cosmic Principle,--the Law of Expansion and Contraction.

The Masters knew the Laws of the Universe. To them the Circle represented Eternity, and the Dot represented the Creative Principle that dwells in a grain of corn, in every living thing, from mustard seed to man.

The Circle has no beginning and no end; and the Dot may be expanded and extended to infinity and contracted to infinity.

These simple, understandable principles constitute the Kingdom of Creation.

Creative processes work in circles, called the Cosmic Cycle. The products are circles. The Universe is composed of Circles. Man's body is composed of circular cells. The cells are composed of circular atoms, and the atoms are composed of electrons which are circles of force.

The atom is composed of an orbit of electrons, revolving round the nucleus in its center, as the planets revolve round the Sun. The electron itself is a whirling force center.

If the material world were seen thru a sufficiently strong magnifying glass it would appear not as a great body of solid, inert matter, but as an aggregation of infinite particles formed into a mass that appears solid to the eye.

But the space between the electrons in the atom is comparatively as great as the space between the planets of our solar system. And every electron, atom and molecule is in constant and intensive action.

Under a glass of sufficient power, nothing solid would be seen in the material world.

If the magnifying glass were increased to infinite power, even the electrons would vanish into seething nothingness, and nothing would appear to be left but the ether, which is imperceptible to the senses even when aided by the strongest instruments in the laboratory of the scientist.

In other words, the apparent solidity of objects is merely relative and comparative.

The Four Principles

Thousands of years of observation and experience show that (1) soil, (2) solar heat, (3) air, and (4) water cover the face of the earth with the vegetal and animal kingdoms.

The Ancient Masters called these the Four Principles of Creation and symbolized them in the Sphinx, in the Four Fixed Signs of the Zodiac, and in the Book of Thoth, the Egyptian Tarot, which has descended to us as a deck of ordinary playing cards.

Card 4 shows the Emperor, seated on a throne, decorated with four rams' heads.

"I am the Great Law," said the Emperor. "I am the Secret Word, the Ineffable Name. The Four Letters of the Name are in me, and I am in everything.

"I am the Four Principles; I am the Four Seasons; I am the Four Quarters of the earth; I am the Four Signs of the Tarot. I am action, resistance, completion, and result.

"For him who has found the way to see me, there are no mysteries on the earth.

"As the earth contains fire, water, and air, as the fourth letter of the Ineffable Name (Yod-He-Vau-He) contains the first three and itself becomes the first, so my scepter contains the complete triangle and bears in itself the seed of a new triangle" (*Mysterious Sphinx*, p. 19).

In all creative processes the Ancient Masters saw that two principles were involved: positive and negative, initiative and receptive, masculine and feminine.

We call this the Law of Polarity; and the law is symbolized in the Tarot by two colors: red and black, while the Four Principles are symbolized by the four suits: Cups (Hearts); Swords (Spades); Wands (Clubs); and Pentacles (Diamonds).

INVISIBLE GASES

With the "splitting of the atom", there dawned a new era that produced the doom of materialism and evolutionism and the rebirth of the invisible world of the Ancient Masters.

The theory of Materialism was shattered by the discovery that Matter, as such, is a myth and has no real existence.

Everything in the Universe is composed of invisible gases in various states of condensation and crystallization, just as the Ancient Masters declared. They said:

"The essence of the Universe is the Infinite Air in eternal motion, which contains ALL in itself. All things are formed by integration and distintegration of the AIR under the law of expansion and contraction."—Anaximenes (380-320 BC).

The invisible gases of the air are the foundation of everything known. That fact leaves the theories of inductive science and material science stranded on the barren rock of empty speculation. These absurd theories had never been born had the fathers of modern theology not destroyed the Archaic Philosophy of the Ancient Masters and admitted it:

39

Archbishop Chrysostom, in the middle of the 5th century A.D., boasted:

"Every trace of the old philosophy and literature of the ancient world has vanished from the face of the earth" (Bible Myths, Doane, p. 436).

Why was that ancient philosophy and literature destroyed? That is a deep secret, well concealed from the masses but now exposed in our various writings, under various titles, which contain The Lost Wisdom of The Ancient Masters.

SEVEN BODIES

According to the ancient philosophy, man has seven bodies or seven grades in what seems to be one body.

Of the seven grades of Being represented in the human microcosm, the three higher ones, the ternary or triad, are noumenal and immortal. These are (1) higher manas or abstract intellect, (2) buddhi or intuition, and (3) atma or pure ego.

This super-phenomenal triad is symbolized in ancient religions by the Sun; and the fabled journey to the Sun is nothing more nor less than a symbolical designation of the process of rendering fully actual the latent potentialities of these three transcendent microcosmic principles.

The four lower grades of Being pertain to the phenomenal order and are technically denominated the quaternary, viz., (1) mental body, (2) astral body, (3) ethereal double (body), and (4) physical body.

These Four Principles of Creation are symbolized in various ways in ancient literature and ancient philosophy. They are the Four Suits of the Tarot and the Four Beings of the Sphinx.

In the Bible they are usually referred to as the Four Beasts, and they are the Four Beasts before the Throne mentioned in Revelation (4:6-9).

In order to mislead and deceive the masses, the biblical references to the Four Principles of Creation appear in sensational descriptions as the Four Living Creatures that came out of the "midst of the fire" (Ezek. 1:4-14); the Four Great Beasts that "came up from the sea" (Dan. 7:2-7); and "these great beasts, which are four, are four kings, which shall rise out of the earth" (Dan. 7:17).

The Bible says the body of man is made of the dust of the ground, but that is wrong (Gen. 2:7). The Ancient Masters never made that statement.

The Bible also says that the breath of God made man a living soul (Gen. 2:7). That is also wrong.

The Bible is wrong again when it says that the life of the flesh is in the blood (Lev. 17:11). That assertion is repudiated by a statement in the New Testament that it is the Spirit which animates the flesh (Jn. 6:63).

The four elements that constitute Man are divided by various authors into the dense body, the water body, the ethereal body, and the solar body. This division is more imaginary than real.

Let us first notice the water body, also called the ethereal double. A pin cannot penetrate the flesh anywhere without drawing fluid from the body. That fluid is composed of blood and lymph, which are liquefied air.

Here are listed the three departments which constitute the dense body; and they are composed of liquefied and solidified air; and air is not the "dust of the ground."

Air is composed of many gases, which are composed of atoms, and which makes the dense body nothing more than an aggregation of atoms.

We now come to the fourth body. Engendering, sustaining, vitalizing, and informing these three departments which constitute the dense body, is the Solar Body, which interpenetrates all substances, causing various rates of vibration in the different densities.

The fourth body, the fire body, the electric body, the astral body, the solar body, the vital force of the body, the life of the flesh, give it any name or designation that you will, is what makes man a Living Soul on the earth plane. And when any obstruction hinders its natural flow and operation, the dense body begins to decline, degenerate, with complete dissolution (somatic death) as the end result.

Because of its supreme importance, the Solar Body shall be noticed in more detail.

Chapter No. 23

THE SUN

The earth, in its great circuit, passes thru the range of a Constellation, represented by a cycle of 2,160 years. During that time, the annual birth of the Sun occurs in the same zodiacal sign.

In each grand cycle of 25,920 years, the earth passes through all twelve houses of the Zodiac, just as the Sun goes thru them in 365.26 days.

The Sun, with its attendant planets, also makes a grand cycle. It, and its family of planets, is moving thru space at a speed of 200 miles a second, traveling around the center of gravity of its cosmic system. At this speed it requires 220,000,000 years to complete just one revolution of its gigantic orbit.

How many times the Sun has circled its orbit cannot even be accurately estimated. Some authorities think it must have made thousands, while others assert that it has made hundreds of thousands.

None of the symbols of antiquity are more important in their signification or more extensive in their application than those of the sun.

The two principal sources of ancient mythology were a wild admiration of the sun and an inordinate respect paid to the memory of powerful, wise, and virtuous ancestors, especially the founders of kingdoms.

To the latter cause we may attribute the euhemerism of the Egyptians, Hebrews, Greeks, and Romans. But in the former we find the origin of sun-worship, the oldest and by far the most prevalent of all ancient religions.

The primeval race of Aryans worshipped the solar orb in his various manifestations as the producer of light and life.

In the Veda there are only three deities: Surya in heaven, Indra in the sky, and Agni on the earth. These three all refer to the same object, the sun, the sky bright from its light, and the fire derived from its rays.

In the profound poetic ideas of the Vedic hymns appear perpetual allusion for the sun with his life-bestowing rays.

Everywhere in the East, amidst its brilliant skies, the sun claimed the adoration of those people. The Persians, the Assyrians, the Egyptians, the Chaldeans—all worshipped the sun.

The Greeks gave a poetic form to the grosser idea and adored Apollo or Dionysius as the sun-god.

In India the Sun was the Great Divinity. The celebrated Labyrinth was built in honor of the Solar Orb. Its twelve palaces, like the twelve super columns of the Temple of Hieropolis, covered with symbols relating to the twelve zodiacal signs, and the occult qualities of the elements, were consecrated to the Twelve Gods or Tutelary Genii of the signs of the Zodiac.

The twelve signs of the Zodiac, as the twelve Great Gods of Egypt, are found everywhere in the ancient world. They were adopted by the Assyrians, the Hebrews, the Greeks, and the Romans.

There is no more striking proof of the universal adoration paid to the Sun, the Stars, and the Constellations, than the arrangement of the Hebrew camp in the Desert and the allegory relating to the Twelve Tribes of Israel, ascribed in the Hebrew legends to Jakob.

The camp was a quadrilateral, in sixteen divisions, or which the central four were occupied by symbols of the four elements; fire, air, water, and earth.

The four divisions at the four angles of the quadrilateral exhibited the four zodiacal signs that the astrologers called fixed, and which they regarded as subject to the influence of the four great Royal Stars, Regulus in Leo, Aldebaran in Taurus, Antares in Scorpio, and Fomalhaut in Pisces, on which falls the water poured out by Aquarius; and of which constellations the Scorpion was represented in the Hebrew blazonry by the Celestial Eagle that rises at the same time with it and is its paranatellon. The other signs were arranged on the four faces of the quadrilateral and in the parallel and interior divisions.

The Vernal and Autumnal Equinoxes the ancients called the Gates to Heaven.

The ancients lamented when, after the Autumnal Equinox, they saw the malign influence of the venomous Scorpion, the vindictive Archer, and the filthy He-Goat "drag" the Sun down toward the Winter Solstice.

Arriving there, they said that he (Sun) had been slain and gone to the realm of darkness.

Remaining there three days, he (Sun) rose again and ascended northward in the heavens to redeem the earth from the gloom and darkness of winter, which was emblematical of evil and suffering; as the Spring, Summer, and Autumn were emblems of happiness and immortality.

The Egyptians personified the Sun and worshipped him under the name of Osiris and transmuted the legend of his descent among the Winter Signs of the Zodiac into a fable of his death, his descent into the infernal regions, and his resurrection. From that fable came the story of the crucifixion, death, and resurrection of the gospel Jesus.

The Egyptians symbolized as gods the stars composing the zodiac, the sub-divisions of the zodiacal signs into decans, the horoscope and the stars that presided therein, and which were termed the Potent Chiefs of Heaven.

Symbolizing the Sun as the Great God, high above all other gods (Ps. 7:17) (etc.) Architect, and ruler of the World, they explained not only the fable of Osiris and Isis, but generally all their sacred legends by the stars, by their appearance and disappearance, by their ascension, by the phases of the moon and the increase and decrease of her light; by the march of the Sun, the division of time and the heavens into dual parts, one assigned to darkness and the other to light.

Clements of Alexandria assures us that the four principal sacred animals, carried by the Egyptians in their processions, were emblems of the four cardinal points of the Zodiac which fixed the seasons at the equinoxes and solstices and divided into four parts the heavenly march of the Sun.

The Egyptians worshipped fire and water and the Nile, which river they styled Father and Preserver of Egypt.

They also revered the other elements; and the Great Gods, whose names are found inscribed on an ancient column, are the Sun, the Moon, the Air, the Earth, night and day. And, in fine, as Eusebius said, they regarded the Universe as a great Deity, composed of a number of gods, the different parts of itself.

This same worship of the Heavenly Host by the Egyptians extended into Asia Minor and prevailed in every part of Europe.

Sun worship is the oldest religious system on earth, and the Bible says "Our God (Sun) is a consuming fire" (Heb. 12:29).

The Psalmist said: Clouds and darkness are round about him (Sun); a fire goeth before him (Sun), and burneth up his enemies. His (Sun's) lightnings enlightened the world; the earth saw and trembled. The hills melted like wax at the presence of the Lord (Sun). The heavens declare his (Sun's) righteous-ness, and all the people see his (Sun's) glory (Ps. 97: 2-6).

The Ancient Masters said: "The Sun illumines all, delights all, from it all proceed, to it all must return; and it alone can irritate our intellects."

Again they said: "All things are the progeny of one fire....For the fire which is first beyond did not shut up his power in matter by works, but by Mind; for the framer of the Fiery World is the Mind of Mind, who first sprarge from Mind, clothing Fire with Fire....The Universe is made of fire and water and

43

earth and the all-nourishing ether."

In his "Primitive History," Williams said: "Noah is the Aion of Nonnus; and Aion is the Sun, with four wings, representing the four seasons."

Modern science takes up the same line of philosophy and teaches that the earth, with all things physical and psychical, which contribute to make the earth what it has been, what it is, and what it is to be, was originally in the Sun and would soon disappear into its original elements but for the Sun.

Every physical and psychical reality which at any time has entered into the earth's history, and that of the other planets, were in that vast, flowing revolving globe of gases, which is said to have been, at one time, at least five billion miles in diameter.

Until comparatively recent times, thru all the theological history of humanity, the sun was almost universally regarded as a god. Manifestly, without it there could be no life on earth; and its annual recurring motions are such as to produce the impression of Birth and Death—of birth by ascension into the heaven of the summer solstice, and of death by descension into the grave of the winter solstice.

The gods of all super-naturalistic interpretations of religion are so many creations of the dominant class, and spurious revelations were put into their mouths by their makers for the purpose of keeping mankind ignorant and contented.

The representations of the Bible concerning the origin and history of man are largely fictitious impositions, not historical compositions.

The God interpolated in the Bible by those who compiled the book for their own use and purpose is not an objectivity. He is a subjectivity existing in the imagination of orthodox Catholics and Christians.

None of the gods of the super-naturalistic interpretations of religions are objectivities. The lesser ones are generally the ghosts of dead men, and the greater ones are versions of the sun myth.

In itself, the sun myth, as symbolism, is not only poetically beautifully but scientifically true. As literalism, it is, in the case of the ignorant, superstition, and in the case of the learned, self-deception or hypocrisy.

All the conscious, personal, creator-gods, destroyer-gods, saviour-gods, and illuminator-gods, with all their angels, heavens, and hells, are so many myths—creations of the imagination, subjective fictions, not objective realities.

The savior-gods are essentially the same mythical personifications of the sun and of the happy events of its annual career because from it the earth, with all the planets, had their origin, and because from it the earth, and all the planets, have the heat, light, and force which makes Life possible.

Henry Salt, eminent English traveller, said: "There is no antiquarian, no inscriptionist, no linguist, but absolutely understands that all historic religions, either thru relics, monuments, or scrolls, have their origin in the sun; and that all ancients, although their religions may be diversified,

44

started on that central pivot....the Sun."

THE PRIESTHOOD

When the priesthood overcame the philosophers at the Nicean Convention in the fourth century A.D., then it made its Bible and put in the mouth of its God this statement:

"Now, therefore, if ye will obey my voice and keep my covenants, then ye shall be a peculiar treasure unto me above all people; for all the earth is mine. And ye shall be unto me a kingdom of priests and an holy nation" (Ex. 19: 5,6).

"Ye shall be named the Priests of the Lord; men shall call you the Ministers of our God; ye shall eat the riches of the Gentiles, and in their glory shall ye boast yourselves" (Is. 61: 6).

These makers of the Bible put in the Old Testament the God of the Jews. This same God is rejected and repudiated in the New Testament.

The Old Testament God had a long discussion with Moses and showed Moses his "back parts" (Ex. chapters 3-14).

The New Testament God is said to be a spirit and that "no man hath seen God at any time" (Jn. 1:18; 4:24).

Then anthropomorphism in time invested the Nature Gods of the ancients with human forms.

When the doctrine was promulgated that the gods were originally men whose virtues had elevated them to the sky, old Bel-Saturn, the oldest and chief god, the Great Spirit of antiquity, would logically be the "First Man."

As the Great Spirit appeared as "First Man," so the biblical Adam, by the doctrine of Euhemerus, was raised to the rank of god. As first god, he was euhemerized into First Man.

In this way the Priesthood disposed of the sun-gods. The Hebrew Priesthood transformed them into Patriarchs. Adam, Ab-Ram, and Israel were names of the Sun.

In the making of their Bible, the Priesthood covered the account of the creation down to Noah's flood in eleven chapters, and then devoted fourteen chapters of Genesis to Ab-Ram, his family and his work.

Ab-Ram was a Chaldean, born in Ur of the Chaldees (Gen. 11: 26, 28). Ur was dedicated to the Moon-God Sin, whence comes the name Mt. Sinai; and Ab-Ram marries Sa-Rai.

The Fire-God of Ur was Ab-Ram. The Hebrew word Ab means Father, and Ram (head sign of the Zodiac) means Most High.

So Ab-Ram, the Fire-God, married Sa-Rai, the Moon-Goddess, and they became the original parents of the Hebrews.

Then later, in order to hide the facts, Ab-Ram's name was changed to

Abraham; and "a father of many nations have I made thee" and Sa-Rai's name was changed to Sarah (Gen. 17: 5, 15).

In his Spirit History of Man, S. F. Dunlap wrote: "Sahra is the Moon....
It was usual with the old Arabians to regard Saturn and Ab-Ram as their progenitors; and while regarding Saturn as their father, they claimed Sahra (Asarah, Asherah, Venus) as their Mother; for the Moon is the Mother of the Kosmos, and the poet wrote that 'all things are born of Saturn and Venus'" (p. 76).

And here is how the world got the biblical Christ. The Hindus called the Sun Chris. The Greeks changed it to Christos; the Romans changed it to Christus; and the English called it Christ the Sun God.

When the Priesthood made its Bible to enthrone the church and enslave the masses, Christ the Son God became Christ the Sun of God.

As late as the sixth century A.D., the words "OUR LORD THE SUN" were preserved in the Christian Liturgy; and it was not until the seventh century that the figure of a man appeared on the Christian Cross.

At the Sixth Ecumenical Council held at Constantinople in 680 A.D., it was ordained that in place of the Lamb the figure of a Man should be portrayed on the Cross; and thereafter the worship of the Lamb on the Cross was prohibited and that of a Man was substituted in its place.

These facts of history demonstrate the evolution of Christianity. The Lamb on the Cross represented Aries, the Head Sign of the Zodiac; and after the Lamb was replaced on the Cross with the figure of Man, the gospel Jesus was then termed "the Lamb of God which taketh away the sin of the world" (Jn. 1:29).

That statement was interpolated in the Bible some time during the seventh century A.D.

In his work titled "Back to the Sun," Dr. Charles Whitby wrote:

"In his dark hour, when doubt, fear, and perplexity are everywhere manifest, it is well to remember that the fate of this earth and its inhabitants is not really at the mercy of our paltry human endeavors.

"To see in our present plight only a meaningless uprooting, levelling, and demoralizing process, without purpose or promise at the center of it, is to be the purblind dupe of illusion" (p. 15).

That darkness, doubt, fear, and perplexity may be laid right at the door of the church, and evidence of this fact appears in the constantly increasing host of unbelievers in the church and in Christendom in general, which is the result of the spread of facts and truth that are uncovering and disclosing the greatest fraud on earth.

ORIGIN OF MAN

It may seem silly and stupid to us for these ancient races to regard the Sun and Moon as their progenitors, and yet many of us consider it sensible and scientific to regard man as an improved ape, the product of evolution,

46

according to the postulate of science.

The dumbest farmer knows that without the Sun, darkness and destructive cold would envelope the earth, and its surface would be as dismal, gloomy, lifeless, naked, and barren as a cobble stone.

That being a fact which even science will not question, it would seem in harmony with law and order that we look for man's origin in the powers of the elements which produce everything that appears on the face of the earth.

We see the products of these powers on all sides and watch them grow and develop as they produce our food and the forests which cover the land.

Is there any reason why we should believe that man is an exception to this law?

In fact, without the Sun, the mythical God of theology would be as helpless as an infant and as impotent as a kitten, and the prayers of the pious would be as futile as the bellow of a bull.

And yet these notorious facts are ignored by science, concealed by the church, and disregarded by the mind-controlled multitude who are taught by their enslavers to look up to a mysterious God in the sky for the source of Creation and the Maker of Man.

Man is the highest of the products which cover the earth, and if man is subject to the laws which govern the Universe, then it is not a difficult problem to discover the source of his origin.

And furthermore, if we come to a correct conclusion, consistency of thought demands that we proceed in our processes in a direct manner thru infinite time to infinite results.

If something cannot come from nothing, then of necessity the characteristics of the something which comes must illustrate and describe with great precision the source from whence it came.

The Microcosm is the product of the Macrocosm and as is the Macrocosm so is the Microcosm. The Macrocosm is of necessity illustrated in the Microcosm; the one, however, infinitely above the other.

The Macrocosm is the Producer and the Preserver; and Like begets Like, in character if not in degree.

The processes of the Microcosm must illustrate, therefore, the processes of the Macrocosm. This requires that the Microcosm must possess the qualities and properties of the Macrocosm.

That which may be known of the Macrocosm is manifest in the Microcosm, and vice versa.

THE MACROCOSMIC GENERATOR

Science shows that the Solar Orb in the sky is the Macrocosmic Generator of the Universe, casting out streams of electrized, intelligized, and polarized electrons which cover the earth with every form of life--the fish of the sea, the fowls of the air, and every living creature that moves upon the earth (Gen. 1:26).

Science shows that Man is no exception to this universal Law. It applies with full force and effect to him, and science declares that he is an electric machine.

At this critical point be not alarmed by this declaration. For Man is not the machine. The evolutionist holds that he is, but the experience and observation of thousands of years prove otherwise.

The Ancient Masters solved this mystery by showing that Man is independent of his body.

Man is that Solar Entity which occupies the Machine and uses it as a vehicle of expression on the earth plane. Keep this point in mind and do not become confused as we proceed.

Leading scientists find, after years of profound study and research, that the human organism is a complicated system of electric batteries, all of them delicately connected with a highly-complicated system of nerves.

The late Dr. George W. Crile, eminent biologist, histologist, physiologist, and surgeon, asserted, after the most exhaustive research, that "each cell in the human body is an electric machine" (Bipolar Theory of Living Processes, 1926).

Prof. H. F. Osborn declared, "We inherit some, if not all, of our physico-chemical characteristics from the Sun; and to that degree we may claim kinship with the stellar universe....since some of our distinctive characteristics and functions are actually the properties of our ancestral star" (the Sun).

Osborn continued: "Physically and chemically we are the child of our great luminary (Sun), which contributes to us all of our chemical elements and all the physical properties which bind them together" (Origin of Life, p. 18).

And Secor, famous electrician, stated that the body is an automatic engine, the functions of which are the result of solar radiation, ruled by intelligence inherent in the cells of the organism.

The harmonious findings, declarations, and conclusions of a score of distinguished specialists in electricity, chemistry, biology, and physiology present incontrovertible facts in support of the postulation that life force, vital force, nerve force, call it what you will, is Solar Electricity.

These scientists found that each cell of the body is a complete bipolar electric mechanism in itself and that the organism as a whole is a complex, bipolar, electric machine composed of many batteries.

RECAPITULATION

1. The Sun, Giant Generator of the Universe, casts out streams of electrized, intelligized, and polarized electrons; and these, under the power of creation inherent in them, cover the earth with all the various forms of living creatures, including Man.

48

2. As the Macrocosm produces the Microcosm, under the law that Like begets Like, the Microcosm must illustrate and describe with perfect precision the characteristics, qualities, and properties of the Macrocosm.

3. As the human organism is constituted of electrized, intelligized, and polarized electrons, it must be an electric mechanism.

4. As the Giant Generator electrizes and vitalizes the Macrocosm.

In "Son of Perfection", we have described and discussed the principal battery of the body, with its seven cells; and in this work we shall show how all the body's batteries are kept charged and how they are connected with the Macrocosmic Generator.

After absorbing our discussion on these vital points, the reader will discover how preposterous is the postulate of science, that Life is the expression of a series of chemical changes, and that vital force is the produce of food. Those who want more on that phase of the subject should read our work titled "The Facts of Nutrition."

SOLAR BODY

It is both interesting and enlightening to observe how the electric, solar body engenders and interpenetrates the other bodies of man.

Man would be amazed could he see the nerve system of his body in its entirety. For it would present to the eye the same size, shape, and form of the dense physical body.

The point of a pin cannot be pressed against the body anywhere without touching a nerve; and the nerves are charged with what modern science calls vital force.

For that force modern science has no definite name nor rational explanation. It is just "food energy," or the result of "chemical action," or "a series of chemical changes," as the great Osler said (Mod. Med. 1907, p. 39).

Let any medical doctor question or attack that theory in public, and he very summarily has his license revoked on the charge of "unethical conduct."

Nerve force, vital force, call it what you will, is Solar Electricity.

During the Life of physical man on earth, the Solar Man and his physical replica present the same identical size, shape, and form, interlaced, interwoven and interblended so perfectly and so completely that in our sight they appear as one and the same, and yet we see only the physical form and little suspect that we are looking at Solar Man when we gaze in a mirror.

Remember, truth is stranger than fiction. The great truths which have shaken society to its center have always appeared insignificant to the superficial observer, while to the discoverer, the Pythagorean philosopher, the Newtonian thinker, the true principle is a pearl of priceless value.

To him who has reached the true vantage-ground of observation by discovering the principle, everything becomes clear, full and obvious. Speculations give way to knowledge and empiricism to the certainty of science. Facts,

49

while otherwise obscure and difficult to be appreciated, are brought near enough to permit of thorough investigation and the consequent attainment of law and order.

Chapter No. 23

Cosmic Radiation

Cosmic Radiation is now a common term; but it has been only a quarter of a century since the late Sir James Jeans, F.R.S., first drew attention to the effect of cosmic rays upon man; whereas, the Ancient Masters had this subject well covered in their astrological system, which was declared worthless by science, but which is now being discovered as a science that goes into the realm of atomism, a field so startling because of its power and force that the world stands amazed and astounded.

Astrology is that ancient science which treats of the effect and influence of the suns and stars of the sky upon the earth and everything on the earth, including the vegetal and animal kingdoms.

In 1939 Prof. P. M. S. Blackett, F.R.S., stated that "the earth (is) being bombarded by atomic particles of surprisingly high energy."

And right here before us, in the confusion of science, like the source of animation, of Life, that strange element which makes man a "living soul;" and yet so completely unknown and unnoticed that the renowned scientist Millikan frankly admitted: "I cannot explain why I am alive." (*Collier's*, Oct. 24, 1925).

In 1951 Edward S. Smith, C.B.E., F.C.S., wrote:

"Cosmic radiation provides the most penetrating rays recognizable at present. The word 'radiation' covers the particles (rays), the electron-volts carried by some of them, and the electro-magnetic waves with which they are associated." (Prana of Yoga, p. 23).

The late Dr. Robert A. Millikan, just mentioned above, was said to have been "the generalissimo of American Science in World War I," and the man who coined the term "Cosmic Rays." He made this observation:

"Cosmic radiation penetrates practically a thousand feet into the earth's crust . . . Cosmic rays reaching the earth at the Equator must contact the earth's magnetic field (aura) as electrons of more than 10 million volts and more than six million volts in latitudes of above 34 degrees north" (*Cosmic Radiation, Colston Papers*, 1949).

The resistance of the earth's electro-magnetic field to cosmic radiation in latitudes of above 34 degrees north is said to equal that of about six feet of lead.

But these scientists overlook the fact that Cosmic Radiation is equal on all portions of the earth's surface. It is only solar radiation that is greater at the Equator and decreases each way from that point toward the poles.

THE EARTH'S AURA

This electro-magnetic field surrounding the earth, called the earth's aura, extends approximately 4300 miles thru to outer space.

When cosmic radiation strikes the centripetal and centrifugal forces of the earth's aura, one of the effects is the creation of the electro-magnetic field, described by Stromberg in his "Soul of the Universe," and referred to by us in Part I of this work.

This field constitutes what occult science calls the Astral World, the world of strange phenomena, the world of the so-called Astral Body of man.

Occult science teaches that the astral body of man is the ethereal body that is capable of projection to a distance. The great Carrel referred to the matter in these words:

"Personality is rightly believed to extend outside the physical contiuum ....Each one of us is certainly far larger and more diffuse than his body.... Obviously, man projects on all sides beyond his anatomical frontiers . . .

"But man diffuses through space in a still more positive way. In tele- pathic phenomena, he instantaneously sends out a part of himself, a sort of emanation, which joins a far-away relative or friend. He thus expands to great distances. He may cross oceans and continents in a time too short to be estimated" (Man, The Unknown, pp. 258, 259, 260).

Another writer says: "When man passes into the Astral Realm and becomes conscious of it, he is then really in the mental body" (Astral World).

In Part I of this work we stated that Stromberg demonstrated by experi- ments that in the electro-magnetic field surrounding the earth there exists the immaterial, invisible entity which expands, develops, and becomes a Living Being, in a physical form on the Material Plane. He said:

"The structure and the functions of a cell, a nerve system, a brain, are not due to the collected molecules of the parts (nor to the food one eats), but to an electrical field of definite properties, structural as well as functional (Soul of the Universe).

There must be structure to function or there could be no function.

The electro-magnetic field, the earth's aura, constitutes that invisible world in which is contained the essence of all that appears in various shapes and forms in this visible world, the Material Plane, comprising both the vegetal and the animal kingdoms.

THE SILVER CORD

In the Bible there appears a strange reference to something that seems to mean little to the clergy and less to the man in darkness. The statement says:

"Or ever the Silver Cord be loosed, or the Golden Bowl be broken" (Eccl. 12:6).

This book of the Bible contains statements found nowhere else in the Old Testament and is not referred to in the New, probably because it so flatly contradicts the fantastic interpolations of those who compiled the Bible from the ancient scrolls.

51

Ecclesiastes means speaker, debater, preacher; and the book contains many sensible statements. It declares that which appears to be mysteries is only natural results from natural causes. That like causes produce like effects; that birth and death are incidents in the plan of events governed by a fixed and never changing power that rolls on forever.

"The book is so different from the rest of the 'Word of God,' and so revolutionary in preachments, the wonder in how the bible builders ever came to make it a part of the bible," wrote Wm. McCarthy, who adds:

"Editors have forged additions and interpolations to give the book a similitude to Proverbs, but fortunately for the truth, these forgeries can be sifted out. As examples, 2:26; 5:3,4,; 7:5,6; 8:12; 12:13,14" (Bible, Church, and God, p. 418).

McCarthy said nothing concerning the Silver Cord and the Golden Bowl in his brief review of Ecclesiastes. The symbology was perhaps overlooked by him. And the statement appears so casual that the priests and preachers have, no doubt, thought it referred to jewelry and ornaments and let it go at that.

Perhaps the Silver Cord was a necklace for the queen and the Golden Bowl was a goblet in which servants prepared special drinks for the king.

Who would ever think that the Silver Cord had any relation to a process of Creation? Or that the Golden Bowl had any relation to man's body?

But these are the very things we should think of if we were taught that Man is the subject of the Bible and that Perfect Man is the Hero of the Bible.

Another strange statement appears in the Bible: "Behold! a door opened in heaven" (Rev. 4:1).

This port of entry into eternal bliss may bear some relation to the Silver Cord. The Cord may be a cable for man to scale in his ascent to his celestial home. Perhaps the gospel Jesus used it when "he was received up into heaven and sat on the right hand of God" (Mk. 16:19).

JAKOB'S LADDER

Then there is Jakob's Ladder. Jakob had a dream in which he saw "a ladder set up on earth, and the top reached to heaven: and behold the angels (were) ascending and descending on it" (Gen. 28:12).

This field of archaic symbology is far too deep for priests and preachers, and to the man in darkness it means just more theological magic and mystery.

We shall see that the Silver Cord and Jakob's Ladder are so intimately related that they represent the same mysterious, biological process in the life of man.

DOOR OPENED IN HEAVEN

We have now approached one of the big secrets of the Ancient Masters, those superstitious heathens of antiquity.

If the things we shall now relate were published before the development

52

of the atomic bomb, the information would have been greeted with doubts and sneers. Even today there are not many who are prepared to believe what we shall say.

From the little-known electro-magnetic field (Astral World) which surrounds the earth, there emerges an invisible current of electric force, discovered by the Ancient Masters and by them called the Silver Cord.

That current they discovered to be the magic Creative Power that covers the earth with the vegetal and animal kingdoms, which we call Nature.

So, according to their doctrine, man was not formed of the dust of the ground and did not become a living soul because a fabulous God puffed into his nostrils "the breath of life." (Gen. 2:7).

That statement is just another of the thousands of interpolations of the men who made the Bible.

Whence comes the forests and flowers which cover the earth? The same earth, the same air, the same water, and the same sunshine are transformed and made to produce all we see in the phenomenal world, of which man is a part.

Is it a greater miracle to produce man than it is to produce all these things by which he is surrounded? Which of all these is the greatest mystery?

Is it a greater miracle to produce thought and will and perception and sensation and all the phenomena of mind, than the colors, perfumes, flavors, fruits, and flowers of the vegetal kingdom?

By, with, and from the Silver Cord the natural world comes into being; and man is a part of it. He is formed by the same creative power, the Brain and Spinal Cord forming first, as if by magic.

The formation results under the law of vibration, by which the invisible becomes visible and the potential becomes actual.

A lawful decrease in the vibratory rate of the Silver Cord transforms the invisible stream of ions and electrons into visible substance, under the same law that transforms invisible vapor into visible water.

The brain of man is formed first and then the region of the skull where the Silver Cord penetrates the brain is called the Fonticulus Frontalis; but to this particular fontanel in the skull medical works pay no especial attention.

In the human fetus there are seven fontanels in the skull. The Fonticulus Frontalis is much the largest and remains open for a considerable time after birth and exhibits a rhythmic pulsation that harmonizes with the beating of the heart.

In fact, we are now at the very core of the great mystery of Life, and yet all medical books contain nothing on this the greatest of all.

The current flowing as the Silver Cord from the electro-magnetic field is that mysterious Vital Force which is responsible not only for the heart's

53

action, but for all the function and pulsation that occurs in the body and for the functions of every organ, gland, and cell.

Scientists wonder as they observe the rhythms of cosmic force but fail to see that these same rhythms appear in all functions of the body and all of them the expression of universal rhythm carried into the body by the Silver Cord.

Medical works are as silent as the grave on this subject and tell us nothing, except that heart action and vital action are the result of nerve force. But what nerve force is we are not told.

The "door opened in heaven," is a spot that is readily felt in the top of the head of a new-born child and called the Fonticulus Frontalis.

The human body is self-conserving in the highest degree. Nothing is in vain. There is reason and purpose in all of its structures and functions, and these are designed by the Master Architect to accomplish definite and specific results. But modern science presents no reason nor purpose for the existence of the Fonticulus Frontalis in the crown of man's skull.

In the biblical allegory, a voice from above comes down thru this aperture in the head, and says: "Come up hither, and I will show thee things which must be hereafter" (Rev.4:1)

What are these things in man's life which must be hereafter? And whence comes the voice? That allegorical mystery we have explained in "Son of Perfection," Part II, p. 25.

We who dig out the Lost Wisdom of the Ancient World, must go way back to the scriptures of the old Masters; termed "superstitious heathens" by modern science and "savages" by theology, to learn about the mysteries of man and to discover the fact that these "heathens" and "savages" knew much about the functions of the body and the secrets of life that are unknown to modern science.

The pious church fathers could not destroy the scrolls of the "heathens" and "savages" of India because the scrolls were so far beyond the reach of their destructive hands.

In those musty scrolls the "door opened in heaven is termed the Brahmarandhra, or the "Aperture of Brahma," the "Throne of Shiva," the "Seat of the Nibodhika Fire," and his fact was known to the church fathers who made the Bible.

To form any conception of the Silver Cord, we must have more knowledge of the body, its constitution, its functions, and its nerve system than modern science has, and that fact is frankly admitted by the great Carrel.

As the stream of Cosmic Electricity penetrates the head, its vibratory rate decreases, and it condenses and materializes into microscopic fibers, piercing the brain in millions of minute threads which meet at that portion of the brain called the medulla oblongata, and there concentrate, converge, and form what becomes the Spinal Cord of the body.

The medulla oblongata, at its lower portion, differs but slightly in size from the Spinal Cord itself, with which it is continuous, but it soon expands in its upper portion and becomes larger.

Medical works describe the brain and some of its functions, but they teach nothing of the functions of the medulla in its relationship to the functions of the brain system.

The nerves proper all originate in the brain, extending down from it in a trunkline called the Spinal Cord with countless nerves branching from the Cord and going to all parts of the body, its organs, and glands.

All the nerves have their specific function and perform it without confusion. If some obstruction hinders the flow of nerve force at any point, the force "burns" its way thru that obstruction--and the painful symptoms arising are given names (diagnosis) by doctors and called "disease." These are "cured" by the administration of poisons that deaden the nerves, thus causing the nerves to lose some of their vital functional powers.

The nerves are diffused thru the brain and interwoven with its substance, making the brain a switchboard that controls the nerves as a telephone or telegraph system.

WHERE PHYSICAL AND ETHERICAL UNITE

We are now at that point in man's constitution where a strange secret occurs and where science gets lost.

As the nerves of the body ascend into the brain as the Spinal Cord, they pass into the medulla oblongata and beyond; and they are said in medical works to end here and there in various parts of the brain.

If this ending of the nerves in the brain is actual, whence comes the life, mind, consciousness, intelligence, vitality, and nerve force of the body? From the brain? Then where does the brain get it? Here let science speak:

"The studies of the physiologist and the physiological chemist abundantly indicate that all vital activities (of the body) are ultimately the expression of molecular rearrangements and combinations. Life is, therefore, the expression of a series of chemical changes" (Dr. Wm. Osler, greatest physician America ever produced, in his Mod. Med. 1907, p. 39).

We should not laugh at this ridiculous, unsound theory of Life. This is the postulate that rules the medical world and leads to the darkness in which science flounders as it attempts to solve the mystery of Life and Man.

This is the message to the world of that science followed by the Freethinkers who have ditched the church God and believe that they are moving forward to the Promised Land of Eternal Bliss under the guidance, as the great Carrel said, of --

"Men of science (who) know not where they are going (and) are guided by chance" (*Man The Unknown*, p. 23).

According to the Ancient Masters, in the brain where science thinks the nerves come to an end is the area where they transform and metamorphose into the invisible Silver Cord.

55

Science thinks the nerves end because they cannot be seen. They simply grow smaller and much finer than the blood capillaries of the body, which were too small to be seen by the aid of the most powerful microscope in 1616, when Dr. Harvey astounded the medical world with his discovery of the circulation of the blood.

Harvey knew that the blood had to go from the arteries to the veins, but he could not explain the mystery.

The nerves do not end. They simply grow smaller and finally dematerialize completely into bluish white rays, converging at the Sahasrara Chakra, the Fonticulus Frontalis in the crown of the head, and there passing out thru the "door opened in heaven" as the Silver Cord.

This is also Jakob's ladder, set up on earth (Spinal Cord in man's body) and the top (Silver Cord) reaching to heaven, the Hindu "Abode of Shiva," with angels ascending and descending.

The angels represent Solar Man entering his terrestrial temple and leaving it. That terrestrial temple becomes a shell when Solar Man leaves it.

The Kundalini Fire of the Yogi is the force that flows in and out of the body over the Spinal Cord and the Silver Cord.

KINGDOM OF THE GOD

The electro-magnetic field hovering over the face of the earth is called the earth's aura. The centripetal and centrifugal forces of this aura form the earth's gravitational field.

From this field there flows thru the Silver Cord and descends on Jakob's ladder, into the human brain and then over the Spinal Cord, the life, vitality, nerve force, intelligence, mind, and consciousness, and all the other qualities which make and constitute physical man.

Sever the Spinal Cord in the neck, and man dies quicker than if shot thru the heart. He dies instantaneously.

On the return trip, ascending Jakob's ladder and passing out thru the "door in the sky," these immortal qualities leave the body thru the Silver Cord—partially in sleep or deep meditation and completely in death.

Life-Mind-Consciousness—these qualities are really one and united they form the Cosmic Unit, the Microcosm, the Ego, the Nous, the Real Man, the immortal Solar Being. They constitute the Kingdom of the God (Lu. 17:21).

When the multitude heard the gospel Jesus preach so much about the Kingdom of (the) God, they thought it must be a wonderful place and asked him to describe it. He did, using the praseology of the Ancient Masters who had preceded him by thousands of years; and this is what he said:

"The Kingdom of (the) God is like a grain of mustard, which, when sown in the earth, is less than all the seeds, but it grows and becomes greater than all herbs" (Mat. 13:31; Mk. 4:31).

Like Solar Man before he extends and expands in the physical body, the kingdom, at first, does not amount to much. But it grows and develops.

How sorely disappointed that multitude must have been by the simple description the gospel Jesus gave of the heavenly kingdom.

Their imagination, like that of modern man is darkness, led them to believe the heavenly kingdom must be the grandest place in the universe, located in a glorious garden of beautiful flowers, with servants and slaves doing the bidding of their Master, who was seated on a Golden Throne and ruled the earth with a rod of iron.

That same man in darkness is due for another disappointment. Truth is always bitter and always hard to swallow.

For the man who has found truth, said the Ancient Masters, new suffering awaits him when he finds the path to Eternity and the understanding of the Infinite (Tarot Card 12, Sphinx, p. 25).

As a Cosmic Unit, the God of the whole earth emerges from the electro-magnetic field, slides down the Silver Cord thru the "door opened in heaven," called the Gateway of the Soul, and descends into the material world, where the God expands, develops, and becomes the greatest mystery in the universe.

Since the decline of the dark ages about three centuries ago, science has been striving to determine what man is and knows no more about him now than it did three hundred years ago.

That great scientist, Alexis Carrel, who kept alive for 27 years a heart fragment of a chick embryo, wrote this description of man:

"Man is made up of a process of phantoms, in the midst of which there strides an unknowable Reality" (*Man The Unknown*, p. 4).

* * * * * * * * * * *

Chapter No. 24

CONSCIOUSNESS

Occult science asserts that Man is just a State of Consciousness. He is that when he enters his body, and he is that when he leaves it.

Consciousness on the physical plane is expressed in the brain as know-ledge which informs us of our existence and our environment.

The unconscious man is only partially alive. He knows nothing on the physical plane and is out of contact with himself as tho he were dead.

There may be contradictory statements in the Bible, as many were engaged in writing the books thereof and they were miles apart; and the translators who prepared the Bible for the church deleted and interpolated to weave in their own thoughts and opinions.

But no statement in the book directly contradicts the assertion that there is an Invisible Power that dwells in the living body, producing the body

57

by the process of expansion and extension and animating it in the state termed life.

In spite of the distortion and interpolation which the ancient writings have suffered, the Bible definitely says: "Know ye not that ye are the Temple of (the) God and that the Spirit of (the) God dwelleth in you," and, therefore, is the real you (1 Cor. 3:16).

That statement is clear and positive and agrees with the facts and observations of daily life—that the Animating Principle of the body, and not the body, is the Real Man.

No effort of study nor any degree of reflection, no matter how long continued, can make man become conscious of a personal identity in himself that is not himself—that is separate from his own body and distinct from his own brain.

That fact is the evidence to prove that the Spirit of (the) God (Solar Man), dwelling in the body, is none other than the Real Man himself.

Thru the nerves, the brain controls the body, all its muscles, organs, and glands. The brain, in turn, is governed from above thru the Silver Cord by Cosmic Consciousness, which we have shown in our work "Son of Perfection" (pt. I, p. 7) to be the Real Man, the Ego, the Nous, the Solar Man.

* * * * * * * * * * * * *

Chapter No. 25

THE HIDDEN ARTIST

In trying to solve the mystery of Life, science has traced the trail of Life down to the smallest visible particle of matter and there found no more to explain the nature of Life than it found in a living man.

Science has shown that the various living forms all start from what appears to be the same identical substance.

Prof. Henry Drummond said: "Take the ovule of the worm, the eagle, the elephant, the man. Let the most skilled observer apply the most searching tests to distinguish one from the other and he will fail.

"But there is something more surprising still. Compare next the two sets of germs, the vegetable and the animal; and still there is no difference. Oak and palm, worm and man all start in life together.

"No matter into what strangely different forms they may afterwards develop, no matter whether they are to live on sea or land, creep or fly, swim or walk, think of vegetate, in the embryo, as it first meets the eye of Science, they are indistinguishable" (Ascent of Man).

Prof. Lionel S. Beale wrote: "There is a period in the development of every tissue of every living thing known to us when they are actually no structural peculiarities whatever—when the whole organism consists of transparent, structureless, semi-fluid bioplasm —when it would be impossible to

58

distinguish the growing, moving matter which was to evolve the oak, from that which was the germ of a vertebrate animal . . . .

"Neither by studying bioplasm under the microscope nor by any kind of physical or chemical investigation known can we form any notion of the nature of the substance which is to be formed by the bioplasm, or what will be the ordinary result of the living."

What appears as the beginning of physical man (body) is termed the Parent Cell, which is said to result from the union of the male and female germ cells.

What does that union really do? It seems to create a condition that activates the Creative Principle, causing it to bring into being what may be termed the Magic Cell, considered as the starting point of man's body.

This primal beginning of man is a mystery to science. Dr. Willard Carver described it thus:

"From the instant of the entrance of the spermatozoon (male element) into the ovum (female element), marked changes occur in its germinal part as well as in that of the male germinal part. These immediately begin a definite state of conduct wholly distinct and different from that so far exhibited. The elements of the ovum approach the spermatozoon in what is termed the zone of attraction, as though welcoming its entrance and attempting to make safe and easy its path of movement.

"The germinal elements, from being concentrated, separate into their particles; and the general cytoplasm of the ovum begins to be organized with relation to what are now called the male pro-nucleus and the female pro-nucleus, and as this arrangement occurs, the gametes or pro-nuclei travel toward each other.

"By the time they come near to each other, certain elements of each stand out separately as though influenced by some electro-magnetic force; and coming nearer, these separate, individiaul particles merge and fuse, as it were, into each other, leaving a clear field in which nothing can be seen. Then, after a period of seeming quiescence, granulation begins to take place at the point occupied by the gametes when they fused and vanished.

"The granulation point is the beginning of the new person and is called the Zygote.

"It will be seen that where the gametes, floating in their fluids, differ from lymph corpuscles, for instance, is at the entrance of the spermatozoon into the ovum.

"Up to that moment, their life history and conduct present nothing different from that of lymph corpuscles. The gametes have been acting in conformity with the vitality animating the male and female organisms in which they were produced.

"But upon impregnation (merging and fusing) all is changed. They cease thus to act and begin to act according to the law of a new vitality and in such manner as to produce a new organism, composed primarily of the material brought from the parents in the gametes. (Note: This last statement is

59

erroneous. H Hotema)

"The temptation to enter the realm of speculation as to what this new vitality is, which manifests itself at this juncture, will be repressed; for it has not yet been given man to know" (*Psycho-Bio-Physiology*, pp. 194-5).

ANALYSIS

1. The male and female elements meet, merge, and fuse, leaving a clear field, in which nothing can be seen.

2. Then, after a period of seeming quiescence, granulation begins to occur at the point occupied by the male and female elements when they merged and vanished.

3. The granulation point is the beginning of the baby, called the Zygote.

4. The particles which begin to form the Zygote present a different mode of conduct and act according to the law of a new vitality.

Carver said that the new vitality began to produce a new organism composed primarily of the material brought from the parents in the gametes.

But that material disappeared from sight, leaving a clear field in which nothing could be seen.

The granulation that later begins to appear in that clear field in different material and exhibits different conduct. It acts according to the law of a new vitality.

This exhibition of different conduct is evidence to show that it is different material and is not the material brought from the parents in the gametes.

Then from whence did it come? We shall see.

The next point is the "new vitality." Its nature and its source Carver refused to discuss, declaring that as yet it had not been given man to know.

The "new vitality" appeared to come from nowhere and assumed with full authority and ability the inexplicable task of producing a new person—the greatest mystery on earth. Cosmic creation working right under our noses.

Beginning its work in the female uterus, in clear, structureless colloid, an unseen power, which appeared to come from nowhere and called the Hidden Artist, begins to perform delicate, definite, intricate processes.

No eye can see it. No science has defined it. When the area is examined under the strongest microscopes, nothing can be distinguished but the structureless colloid.

What is this invisible agency? Of it Drummond said, "The Artist who operates upon matter in this subtle way and carries out his law—is LIFE!"

But we are still in the dark. That tells us little. What is Life? What its nature and whence its source?

Drummond further observed:

"To understand that it is really the Potter who does the work, let us follow a description of the process by a trained observer, Prof. Thomas H. Huxley. Thru his microscope he is watching the development, out of a speck of protoplasm of one of the commonest animals: 'Strange possibilities,' says he, 'lie dormant in that semi-fluid globule.'

"The plastic matter undergoes changes so rapidly and yet so purposeful in their succession that they can be compared with the work of an expert modeller upon a lump of soft clay.

"As with an invisible trowel, the mass is divided and subdivided into smaller and smaller particles until it is reduced to an aggregation of granules not too large to build the finest fabrics of the nascent organism.

"And then, it is as though an invisible finger traced out the line to be occupied by the brain and spinal cord and to proceed with its work so artistically that, after watching the process hour by hour, one is possessed of a notion that some stronger aid to vision than an achromatic would reveal the hidden artist, with his plan before him, working with skillful manipulations to perfect his task."

It is highly important to observe here that the first parts of the body to be formed are the brain and spinal cord.

The formation of the entire body results from the transformation of the invisible elements flowing in thru the Silver Cord, and the point of that primary transformation appears right here in the visible formation of the brain and spinal cord.

Carver's "new vitality," the nature and source of which he refused to discuss and which Drummond called Life, is the Key to the entire mystery of Man, of Life, of Soul and Eternity.

Solve that secret and there is nothing covered that shall not be revealed; and nothing hid that shall not be known (Mat. 10:26).

Solve that secret and the theological mystery of the Soul, of heaven, hell, and salvation, is evaporated, dissipated, pulverized, and reduced to harmless, worthless dust, and no longer will sermons and preachers be needed to guide the helpless masses thru the wilderness of confusion, perplexity, doubt, and despair, to the Promised Land of Eternal Bliss, where there shall be no more night, no more tears, no more death, neither sorrow nor crying--for the former mystery and confusion of the church are passed away (Rev. 21).

THE NEW VITALITY

1. This New Vitality which seems to come from nowhere, and which Carver said it has not been given man to know, is Drummond's "Life," flowing thru the Silver Cord from the electro-magnetic field and--

2. The Hidden Artist that appears to do the creative work is the inherent power of the electrized, intelligized, and polarized elements of the Universe, not composed of the used material brought from the parents in the gametes, but

61

new, fresh material coming from the electro-magnetic field and flowing thru the Silver Cord and possessing the qualities and properties which abide in every part, particle, electron, and ion of the Universe, and which build everything on the earth and appear to be the same, whether for an oak tree or for a medical doctor.

THE MAGIC WORK

Let the great Carrel describe this magic work called Creation. He wrote:

"An organ builds itself by techniques very foreign to the human mind. The organ is not made of extraneous material like a house. Neither is it just a cellular construction, a mere assemblage of cells.

"It is, of course, composed of cells, as a house is composed of bricks. But it is born from a cell, as if the house originated from one brick, a magic brick that would set about making other bricks.

"Those magic bricks, without waiting for the architect's drawings, or for the coming of the workers, would assemble themselves and form the walls. They would also metamorphose into window-panes, roofing-slates, coal for heating, and water for kitchen and bathroom.

"An organ develops by means such as those attributed to fairies in the tales told to children. It begins as a call and is engendered by cells, which, to all appearances, have a (previous) knowledge of the future edifice and synthetize from substances contained in blood plasma the building material and even the workers" (*Man The Unknown*, p. 108).

GOD OF CREATION

We have now reached that point where the reader should don his best clothes and his best deportment, for we are going to lead him directly up the aisle to the very Throne of God and shock him by showing that he is actually the Temple of God and that the Spirit of God dwells in him, as the Bible says (1 Cor. 3:16).

Carrel cleared up the mystery of Drummond's Hidden Artist; but there is still some question as to the source of the material of which the new organism is built and which Carver assumed came primarily from the parents in the gametes.

1. The Hidden Artist, called Life by Drummond, abides right in the material itself. The Hidden Artist is not a separate, distinct entity as Drummond assumed, but is shown by Carrel to be the electrized, intelligized, and polarized properties inherent in the building material.

2. And that Hidden Artist is the Master Architect of the Cosmos, the Creator of the Universe, the anthropomorphic God of the church.

3. Christianity says: "By a paradox which defies the reasoning faculties, but which is readily resolved intuitively, God is said to be apart from, and independent of, the universe, and yet to permeate every atom of it" (p. 9).

And we have shown you here, Mr. Catholic and Mr. Christian, that your mysterious God does permeate every atom of the Universe, not as a personal entity but as a cosmic force.

4.   Carrel erred when he assumed that the building material, in which the Creative God dwells, is composed of the used and second-hand elements synthetized from substances contained in blood plasma.

5.   Those substances are the used elements which have served their purpose and given up their creative properties. They are not the new, primal, fresh material from the electro-magnetic field which enters into the construction of the new body, the "future edifice" as Carrel called it.

6.   The used elements are what Carver said was "the material brought from the parents in the gametes."

7.   Cosmic Creation does not use second-hand material in building new bodies. That new building material comes not from the parents nor from the blood plasma, but from the electro-magnetic field, as we have said.

THE CHEMICAL FACTORY

Now we shall notice another important point which shows how modern science is lost in the jungles of confusion.

According to the eminent Dr. Berman, the "Hidden Artist" mentioned by Drummond seems to work like this:

"Our chemical factory consists of cells (which we have been discussing), manufacturing special substances that act upon the other cells of the body and so start and determine the countless processes which we call life. Life, body and Soul emerge from the activity of the magic ooze of their silent chemistry."

In explaining and analyzing the properties of Life and Soul, that statement is just as logical and enlightening as the statements of preachers, as they describe the glories of God's kingdom, the powers of Christ, and the mysteries of the Soul.

Drummond assumed that Life was a distinctive entity, but Berman says it is not. It is just the processes of the body. That is exactly what the great Osler said.

And the Soul, that strange entity which, according to the church, is either SAVED OR LOST, depending on one's "belief," "emerges as a process from the activity of the magic ooze of the cells' silent chemistry."

From whence came the cells of Berman's factory? And how did they become organized to form his factory? These are minor details which he deems are too unimportant to be noticed. But after he gets his magic factory organized and in operation, then great things happen, and the mysteries of Life are solved.

Those who desire to follow further this line of thought should read our work titled "Facts of Nutrition."

Man's body is not built of food as science teaches, but of cosmic elements that flow from the electrical field; and man himself, the Ego, is the

63

life force, vital force, nerve force, which penetrates the body thru the brain, spinal cord, and nerve system.

The Life Force, also termed the Life Principle, is the Solar Body that interpenetrates all the substances which constitute the physical body, causing various rates of vibration in the different densities.

The chief seat of the Ego is said to be in the frontal sinus of the head (Golden Bowl) and is termed the Throne of the Divine Man and symbolically re-ferred to in the Bible as the Throne of the God and of the Lamb (Rev. 22:1).

When the church fathers interpolated that statement in their Bible, they knew it did not mean what the church teaches the masses it means.

PROOF OF PRE-EXISTENCE

We stated in Part I of this work that Stromberg experimentally studied the electro-magnetic field to see whether there was any surrounding a tadpole.

Now the church, of course, would seriously object to having man lowered to the level of a tadpole; but if God makes everything, there is bound to be a definite relationship between everything that God makes and has made.

So, with a super-sensitive electrical instrument, Stromberg explored the field in the water surrounding the tadpole. The effect was startling when the animal was undergoing the metamorphic process-changing from tadpole to frog.

He discovered that the structure of the future animal was already in ex-istence as in invisible form before it had acquired a material substratum. The immaterial form was present before the molecules had become incorporated in the material structure.

Stromberg put the mystery in these words: "The substance, which was the Soul (of the animal) in solution, clicked into place, and the animal came into (visible) being" from the invisible world.

But according to the church, man is the only being on earth that has a Soul. God did not give other creatures a Soul. Nor did the form of man have a soul, according to the Bible made by the church fathers, until God puffed "into his nostrils the breath of life," and then "man became a living soul" (Gen. 2:7).

Stromberg's experiments showed that the immaterial form, the Potential Being, not only exists before the material form appears, but that it remains after the material form is gone, disintegrated, and returned to the original elements.

MAN RAISED IN INCORRUPTION

These discoveries of advanced scientists prove the soundness of the ancient doctrine regarding the Pre-Existence of Man as a pure, celestial Being.

And so the Bible says, "We are incorruptible . . . . It (the body) is sown in corruption; it is raised in incorruption. In a moment, in the twinkling of

64

an eye . . . the dead (Solar Man in the physical body) shall be raised incorruptible, and we shall all be changed. For this corruptible (physical body) must put on incorruption (Solar Body), and this mortal must put on immortality.

"So when this corruptible shall have put on incorruption and this mortal shall have put on immortality, then shall be brought to pass the saying that is written, Death is swallowed up in victory. O death, where is thy sting? O grave, where is thy victory?"--Is. 25:8; Hos. 13:14; 1 Cor. 9:25; 15:42, 52-55).

There is nothing puzzling about these biblical statements when properly presented and the underlying principle is explained and understood.

Lactantius said that the Masters could not conceive how it were possible that Man should exist after the demise of his body if he did not exist before, i.e., if his true nature were not independent of the physical body.

* * * * * * * * * * *

Chapter No. 26

THE LIFE LINK

The Silver Cord may be very appropriately compared to the umbilical cord that links the embryo to the mother.

For it is the Cosmic Cord that links the physical body to the astral body, which Paul called the spiritual body (1 Cor. 15:44).

It is the Cosmic Cord that links the Microcosm to the Macrocosm; that links the Son to the Father; that links the Product to the Producer. And we have said that the qualities of the Product describe with great exactness the qualities of the Producer.

Man, the peak of all creation, contains within himself all the powers, systems, planets, and globes of the universe. The cells of his body are Suns composed of electrized, intelligized, and polarized atoms, and the atom itself is a tiny universe.

Man's body is a mass of millions of suns, stars, planets, organized into systems of cells, molecules, atoms, and electrons, all revolving in the body at terrific speed; and that propelling power is not the product of food nor the expression of molecular rearrangements and combinations nor of a series of chemical changes, as stated by the greatest physician that America has produced.

That power emanates from the electro-magnetic field described by Stromberg, and that field is produced by solar radiation.

We can form a better conception of the Silver Cord by thinking of a radio beam that extends for miles into the ether and along which airplanes may be guided accurately and safely.

In the fables for children, the fairies slide down a moonbeam. These ancient fables and myths usually deal with profound secrets of life.

Man can direct pilotless planes and control guided missiles by a phase of

65

electricity called radio and radar, but little suspects that his own body is produced, developed, preserved, directed, and controlled by a phase of solarical electricity called the Silver Cord.

Dr. Beale made some interesting observations on the Silver Cord. He said:

"There have been many cases, even in the knowledge of this writer, where patients have left their bodies and were able to look down on the unconscious shell (their body) from above.

"In such experiences, the complete entity (mind, astral brain, and other parts of the solar body, all in fact) is separated or extracted or evulsed from the physical shell and yet remains anchored to it by a tenuous cord of astral substance, by means of which the entity is able to return to and activate the shell again, provided the cord is not broken.

"But should this cord for any reason snap or sever, then such person would be reported as "dead," and his body would be dead.

"This is not imagery, for, apart from the stated experience of the person himself, were a trained occultist, or even a clairvoyant, present at the time of the phenomena, he would be able to see and describe the comatose physical body and the divorced or separated entity hovering over it, joined by the (silver) cord (like an umbilical cord of the new-born child)" (*Evolution of Mind*, pp. 45, 46).

In Part I of this work, we described the dying process, stating that man, as he leaves his body, can see his body and also a dim haze between him and his body.

That dim haze is described by some as the body's aura. This is erroneous, for the aura disappears at death.

That dim haze is the Silver Cord which contains the Ego, the Cosmic Unit, the Real Man; and he looks out thru it as one looks thru a fine veil over one's face.

Like a radio beam, the Silver Cord is capable of practically infinite extension. In sleep we may, as in dreams, leave the body thru the "door opened in the sky" and fly miles away, yet the body remains alive and we return to it--as long as the Silver Cord remains intact. But when the Cord breaks, death of the body immediately ensues.

This fact strongly indicates that Life is transmitted to the body thru the Silver Cord. But some authors hold that it flows into the body from the Sun and is absorbed by the spleen, where it is divided into seven streams of vital force and directed along the nerves to the various etheric centers.

This theory appears to be mere speculation, with no foundation in fact.

THE PROCESS OF DYING

Death frightens the ignorant and the intelligent only who believe what the church teaches.

It is as natural to die as to be born. Dying is painless. It is like passing out of darkness into the dawn of day. It is a physiological process as natural as breathing and as painless as eating.

A certain doctor wrote: "The moment immediately preceding death from disease is that of utter insensibility to all pain, or of a delightful passivity, or of the complete relaxation of all things pertaining to the physical condition."

As the life force fades from the external portions of the body and concentrates in the vital interiors, one suddenly remembers having gone thru the same experiences in antecedent incarnations. This state results from the fading out of the objective mind as our consciousness passes to the subjective mind.

As the life force fades still more from the external portions of the body and concentrates into the deeper exteriors, there is a pleasant relaxing sensation, due to gradual parting of the etheric fibers as this portion of the body disengages itself from the numerous nerve fibers of the physical body.

Slowly the body sinks into that profound sleep from which it never awakens again.

That is the end of the natural function by which Solar Man is liberated from the body in the "Born Again" process. That is the end of the state of consciousness that manifests in the body.

In the dying process, the Spinal Cord weakens as the life force flows out over the Silver Cord and fails to return.

If the life force flows out over the Silver Cord, it must flow in thru the Silver Cord; and the Spinal Cord weakens because the body, for certain reasons, cannot consume the inflowing vitality.

This would cause a weakening of the Spinal Cord up to the point where it joins with and becomes the Silver Cord, with actual death of the body ensuing when the weakened link between the two sections blew out like a fuse.

To recapitulate: The Cosmic Unit expands and extends until it forms the material man. Then we may follow it in the reverse order, where it shrinks and contracts, leaving the visible body and returning to the invisible realm.

The Solar Body (Cosmic Unit) interblends and interpenetrates with the physical body, supporting and supplying it with all the qualities that sustain terrestrial life.

In the physiological process called death, all that happens to the Ego, Solar Man, Cosmic Unit, is a change of consciousness from its focal point in the material body to the focal point in the Solar Body.

For a split second at the moment of death, the Solar Body can see the replica of the physical body while the state of consciousness is fading and changing from the material body to the Solar Body.

The Seers and Masters had developed the power to liberate themselves voluntarily from their body, and such cases are mentioned in the Bible as follows: "I was in the Spirit in the Lord's Day" and "immediately I was in spirit" (Rev. 1:10; 4:2).

LEAVING THE BODY

In referring to the dying process, Dr. Charles Whitby said, "The experience of getting out of the body has been described by one who recovered from a death-like swoon as like struggling thru a dark, narrow tunnel into a broad, brilliantly lighted place.

"How similar this is to man's being born in the flesh. The typical experience of the infant during and immediately after the process of being born of the mother" (Back to the Sun, p. 114).

In the dying process, everything becomes clearer. The mind becomes more lucid than ever before; the head becomes intensely brilliant, like a glittering Golden Bowl.

The Masters knew what they were doing when they called the Skull the Golden Bowl (Eccl. 12:6).

At the same time the Silver Cord grows stronger to protect the Ego; and "the etheric body," says one author, "flows out thru the Cord like a rapidly moving fluorescent light, imperceptibly extracting the body's vitality more and more, somewhat as a suction, and the Ego passes out of the body thru the top of the head as a radiant etheric light" (Cosmic Fire, p. 86).

That is a description of the dreaded, terrifying physiological process of dying, which is all over, says the Bible, "in the twinkling of an eye" (1 Cor. 15:52).

That is the true interpretation of the biblical "born again" mystery (Jn. 3:3, 5, 7).

That is the mysterious CHANGE mentioned in the Bible in which the "dead" is "raised incorruptible," and the sting is taken out of death, and the grave loses its victory over life (1 Cor. 15: 51-55).

Verses 56-58 of that chapter of 1st Cor. were never written by Paul. They are spurious interpolations, inserted by the church fathers to bring their "Lord Jesus Christ" into the picture, to increase the confusion, and to deceive the masses.

THE COSMIC UNIT

We have described the Four Principles of Creation and shown that man's body is constituted of these four principles.

We come now to the Cosmic Unit which emerges from the electro-magnetic field, flows down the Silver Cord thru the "door opened in heaven," called the Gateway of the Soul, and appears on earth as Man.

The Cosmic Unit is composed of Four Seed Atoms, corresponding to the Four Principles and each principle having its own Seed Atom in the Unit.

The Cosmic Unit is the eternal Ego which leaves the body thru the top of the head in the death process and appears as "a radiant etheric light" that

68

can be seen by the true Clairvoyant.

During the dark ages, some of those so unwise as to say they could see that Light were burned by the church as "witches." Even today those who can see that Light had better keep the secret to themselves.

The Seed Atoms are described as vortices of force revolving at terrific speed, each forming a nucleus around which the four bodies of man are built by the accumulation of atoms, and man comes into visible existence.

The Cosmic Unit of Four Seed Atoms is so small that it would require a group of a million to form a speck visible under the most powerful microscope.

The experiences passed thru by man in his earthly life are impressed upon the Seed Atoms like a message on a phonograph record, making it possible for the hypnotist to have his subject describe events that occurred during antecedent incarnations.

While the other atoms of the dense body have been renewed from time to time, the Seed Atoms forming the Cosmic Unit have remained fixed and permanent.

The Cosmic Unit remains stable not only thru one life, but it remains stable and has been a part of every dense body ever used by that particular Ego.

That Cosmic Unit is the creative agency of the universe.

The Cosmic Unit leaves the dense body at death and returns again at the dawn of another physical life to serve as the nucleus around which is built the new dense body to be used by the same Ego.

That is the Doctrine of Reincarnation as taught by the Ancient Masters, who claimed that they had the evidence to prove the truth of their teachings.

When the Cosmic Unit is ready to leave the dense body, the Silver Cord does not break until the panorama of one's past life has been etched into the Seed Atoms.

LIFE AFTER DEATH

There is a wealth of literature on the subject of survival after death; and if we survive after the death of the body, we were in existence before we were born in the flesh.

In that very ancient work called the *Book of the Dead*, said to have been written by the Egyptian Thoth, it is said that the god-man Osiris had the power to be born again and to look down on his body at death. That he could give life because he was life; that he could make man to rise from the dead because he was the resurrection.

On the wall of the ancient Egyptian temple of Denders appeared the Zodiac Circle and a group of scenes depicting the death and resurrection of Osiris, who says: "I am the resurrection and the life" (Budge, vol. 2, pp. 126, 141, 312).

69

Modern preachers don't know that it was there where the church fathers found these statements, which they put in the mouth of their character called Jesus when they made their Bible (Jn. 11:25).

Numerous cases have been cited of persons who have been out of their body and gazed down upon it while undergoing an operation or when on the verge of dying and recovered.

In Fate Magazine of October-1953, Margaret Linden gave an interesting account of passing out of her dense body and returning to it again. She was ill and rushed to a hospital for an operation. Not more than a couple hours after the operation, she said:

"I was back in bed and was reviving from the effect of the anaesthetic and heard myself crying over and over, 'Don't send me back!'

"I can further remember trying frantically to move my inert body and of being restrained by the doctor, who held both my hands.

"He was speaking quietly, insistently, striving to impress on my subconscious that it must hold fast to the remembrance of why I was begging 'not to be sent back.'

"The next day when I returned to full consciousness, the doctor was there and asked me, 'Did I remember?'

"I did, and I do now.

"At some time during the operation, I--my spirit--left my body. I was flying, and I knew this was no dream. For I had died. I knew it, and I welcomed it.

"It was far more wonderful than any dream. I was no longer imprisoned in my body. I was lighter than thought; I had no weight, no substance at all. I knew I was no longer a (physical) person.

"I was just an essence, a vital spark, equipped with thoughts, feelings, and senses. The feeling above all else was that of extraordinary happiness.

"I could hear magnificent music, and it seemed that I was the center of it.

"As I was savoring this ecstasy in its entirety, a voice in me commanded: 'You must go back; you must go back.'

"And I felt as if I were being pushed downward. I cried, I implored, but again came that command: 'You must go back.'

"Down I came, faster and faster, until, with a crash, I felt myself pushed into what seemed to be a box of lead, which my spirit knew was my body.

"After I told this to the doctor, he informed me that toward the end of the operation I had no pulse, no heart beat, no breath. I was apparently dead. He had immediately inserted his fingers through the incision in my body and was able to massage my heart, hoping to start its action.

70

"He succeeded--and I was alive again."

THE COMMON ERROR

When the Silver Cord is loosened and the Real Man has been released from his dense body, a moment of the highest importance comes to the Ego, and it cannot be too strongly impressed upon the friends and relatives of a dying man that it is a crime against the departing Ego to give expression to loud grief and lamentation, for it is just then engaged in a process of supreme importance; and a great deal of the value of the past life depends upon how much attention the Ego can give to this matter.

It is also a crime against the dying to administer stimulants which have the effect of forcing the higher vehicles back into the dense body with a jerk, thus imparting a great shock to the dying man.

It is no torture to pass out, but it is torture to be dragged back into the dense body, to endure further suffering.

Some who have passed out have told investigators that they had, in that way, been kept dying for hours and had prayed that their relatives would cease their mistaken kindness and let them die.

* * * * * * * * * * *

THE SAHASRARA

In our work titled *Son of Perfection*, we presented the secret of the body's Electric Battery with its Seven Cells, called Chakras by the Hindus.

According to the Hindu doctrine, these Chakras are differing centers of consciousness and vitality. The sixth is said to be the center of the subtle mental principle; and the seventh, the Sahasrara, while not properly a Chakra, is called the abode of Shiva and also the Brahmarandhra, the "hole of Brahma," or the soft spot in the crown of a baby's head.

In the skull there are seven areas between the bones called fontanelles. The largest is the fonticulus frontalis and is easily felt in the fore part of the top of the head in the new-born child. It exhibits a rhythmical pulsation.

This is the point where the Silver Cord penetrates the Golden Bowl (head).

The ossifying process going on in these bones spreads to the fibrous membrane of the fonticulus frontalis, and the aperture is usually closed between the second and fifth years, but in some cases it never closes.

In honor of this sacred spot, which has been poetically expressed as a "window into space," the monks of all ancient nations shaved off the hair over this spot which is supposed to look into the sky.

All writers on Yoga have translated Brahma-Randhra as "hole." The term could better be translated "cavity."

In the ancient Sanscrit, this port of entry was called "the gateway of

71

the Soul," and is the natural point of ingress and egress.

This cavity, the abode of Shiva, is the positive, masculine principle of creation. In its inner center is the mystic Great Void worshipped by the Devas in secret (the Nigruna Shiva within the Parabindu).

In this cavity the female creative principle (Kundalini Shakti) meets and unites with its opposite (Shiva) after its ascent thru the chakras of the spinal column from the generative center at the base of the spine.

This union is mentioned in the Bible as "the marriage of the Lamb" (Rev. 19:7) and is falsely presented by theology to make it appear as the marriage of the gospel Jesus and the church.

In the Sahasrara, according to the Ancient Masters, occurs the mysterious transformation of the etheric Silver Cord to the physicalistic Spinal Cord of the material body of man. This is the point where the invisible Solarical Man becomes or inters the visible physical man.

The Silver Cord and the Spinal Cord are actually one, being a continuation of each other, with the visible portion in the visible body and the invisible portion in the invisible body.

At the lower end of the Cord, in the visible body, is the creative power of man in the visible world; and at the upper end of the Cord, in the electro-magnetic field discovered and described by Stromberg, is the creative power in the invisible world.

This is the secret of the Silver Cord, so closely guarded by the Ancient Masters.

This is another secret of the body's constitution about which modern science knows nothing.

The great Carrel declared that "immense regions of our inner world (of our body) are still unknown" (*Man The Unknown*, p. 4), and this is one of them.

GATEWAY OF THE SOUL

As stated above, the "Door opened in the Sky" is the entrance into the intercommunicating cavity of the four ventricles of the brain and is continuous with the central canal (Chitra) of the Spinal Cord, in which is located the mysterious Sushumna nadi, strangely symbolized in the Bible as the gospel Jesus crucified between two thieves (Jn. 19: 17, 18).

Occult students know that the two thieves represent the Ida and Pingala nadis, as we have explained in *Son of Perfection*; while Jesus, as we explained in that work, represents the Sushumna nadi, called that "wonderful Nature Ray" by Dr. Beale (*Evolution of Mind*, p. 53).

The Cosmic Fire in the generative region at the base of the spine, when conserved and not consumed in masturbation or copulation, ascends thru the Sushumna to the brain and flows thru the cavity to the Gateway of the Soul; and in such cases those who developed the power to liberate themselves voluntarily from their body are mentioned in the Bible as being in the Spirit.

And so Apollonius said, "I was in the Spirit in the Lord's Day," and "immediately I was in the Spirit" (Rev. 1:10; 4:2).

Just what occurs in such instances? It is all very simple when the principle is understood: Only a change of Consciousness.

All that happens when man dies is just a change of Consciousness, from its focal point in the material body to the focal point in the Solar Body.

It is not necessary for man to die in order to produce this change. In the Ancient Mysteries the neophyte was taught how to do it. He was instructed in the secret of how to black-out the Objective Mind entirely and let himself relax and sink completely into the control of the Subjective Mind.

That was what Apollonius did, and he termed it being in the Spirit.

In that case man rises to the fourth dimensional plane and liberates himself from all physical limitations of the five senses, which changes the focal point of his consciousness from the material to the Solarical Body.

And for that period of time man is omniscient: Solid objects become transparent and may be seen inside and out, past and future, space and time, disappear, and become the eternal present (*Son of Perfection*, Pt. II, p. 89)

All of this means that while the Ego is still attached to the dense body by the Silver Cord, the Ego rises superior to the earth plane, as in the case of the true Clairvoyant, or leaves the body as one does in dreams and enters the fourth dimensional plane (invisible world) and yet is attached to the body by the Silver Cord, which is capable of practically infinite extension, as we have said.

This was one of the top secrets of the Masters, and details of the principle involved were never committed to writing, save in the deepest symbolism, as in the case of the last book of the Bible, which we have interpreted in *Son of Perfection*.

Manly Hall has described the rising Cosmic Fire as follows:

"In the disciple, this force can be seen ascending the spine with a glow of light, which finally protrudes from the crown of the head (at the Fonticulus Frontalis) in the form of a long pencil-like shaft" (*Super Faculties*, p. 36).

This protruding shaft of Radiant Etheric Light, visible to the true Clairvoyant, is a portion of the Silver Cord, rising from the "door opened in heaven," and by Beale termed a "Stream of Consciousness" (*Evolu. of Mind*, p. 54).

That protruding shaft of Etheric Light is Solar Man (Soul of Man), constituted of Four Seed Atoms.

We can understand that smallness means little since we have been shown the terrific power of the hydrogen bomb, with more powerful bombs yet to come.

Material Science and the Evolutionists assert that man has no Soul; and here the Soul appears in a form that it is possible for the true Clairvoyant to see.

THE NECTAR OF LIFE

The lining membrane of the important brain cavity leading to the Gateway of the Soul is continuously excreting a precious fluid called the Nectar of Life, mentioned in the Bible as—

A river of the Water of Life, clear as crystal, flowing out of the throne of the God (Golden Bowl, Brain, Skull); and on each side of the river was the Tree of Life, producing twelve fruits according to the months, each yielding its fruit; and the leaves of the tree were for the healing of the people—and the accursed (function of animalistic propagation) shall be no more (Rev. 22:1-3).

The generative function of the physical body, which consumes the Creative Cosmic Essence at the base of the spine, is strictly nothing but an animal function and can never be anything else.

The functions of the physical body are left in that body by the Solar Body, and in the Solar Body this "accursed" function does not exist. The only true creative function is that of the Nous, the solarical faculty of Formative Thought.

Of the precious cerebro-spinal fluid which the Masters called the Nectar of Life, Dr. A. T. Still, Father of Osteopathy, wrote:

"All nerves drink from the waters of the brain . . . The cerebro-spinal fluid is the highest known element in the human body" (*Philosophy of Osteopathy* 1899).

The Nectar of Life, also called the Golden Oil in the Bible (Zech. 4:12), is the Water of Life excreted by the brain (Throne of the God) and flows down the Spinal Cord to the Solar Plexus (cave, manger—Lu. 2:4), and there it is activated by the Sun (Helios, Holy) Breath (Ghost), and the Seed (Son) is born.

Every 29½ days (month) in the life of man and woman after puberty, when the moon is in the sign the Sun was in at the time of one's birth, there is a psycho-physical Seed (fruit) born in the Solar Plexus, which in the ancient text is termed "House of Bread," because it lies behind the stomach.

So, Jesus was born in Bethlehem (Mat. 2:1). Bethlehem is from Beth, House, and Lechem, Bread; and Jesus thus became the "Bread of Life which came down from heaven (brain) (Jn. 6:35, 41).

Water symbolizes the body fluid that carries the Seed, with the fishy odor. So it was in order for the disciples to be fishermen, working around the water. The early Christians used a Fish as their secret sign.

After birth, Jesus is taken down into Egypt. This represents the descent of the Seed into the dark, lower part of the body, symbolized by the Masters as Egypt, which was called the "Land of Darkness"; and there it remains until the neophyte subdues his epithumetic nature, symbolized in the Bible as the death of Herod. Then "Out of Egypt have I called my Son" (Mat. 2:14, 15).

At the end of the brain cavity leading to the Gateway of the Soul, there is an orifice which connects what the Yogi call the internal cavity of Prana with the external cavity of Akasha, surrounding the brain and Spinal Cord, and termed the sub-arachnoid space, which is bathed in the Nectar of Life.

According to Yoga, the Sun is the kama-rupa, or desire body, of Akasha, the second aspect of Brahma (*Cosmic Fire*, p. 1046).

THRONE OF LIBERATION

The Yogins term the Sahasrara Chakra (door opened in heaven) the Throne of Liberation of Solar Man from his terrestrial Prison, thru the Silver Cord.

According to Yoga, the Sadhaka who has known the mystic Great Void of the Sahasrara, is freed from rebirths (Samsara). He cannot be bound in any of the three worlds, the physical, ethereal, and astral. He is forever free of his earthly poison and can fly thru the sky at will.

Heat, cold, fire, and water have no effect on Solar Man.

An interesting allegory in the Bible, not understood by the clergy, refers to these mysteries in these words:

"After this I looked and, behold, a door opened in heaven: and the first voice which I heard said . . . Come up hither, and I will show thee things which must be hereafter.

"And immediately I was in the spirit; and, behold, a throne was set in heaven, and (the God) sat on the throne.

"And he that sat (on the throne) was to look upon like an opal and a carnelian, and a rainbow encircled the throne in appearance like an emerald" (Rev. 4: 1-3).

We have described the "door opened in heaven." The "throne set in heaven" is the protruding shaft of colorful etheric light, Solar Man himself; and it was he that sat on the throne.

The colors surrounding Solar Man and the throne were the electrical emanations of Solar Man and the Silver Cord.

"I will show thee things which must be hereafter" refers to a peculiar blending of the powers of seeing and hearing that occurs when Solar Man is liberated from the limitations of his five senses, as we have explained in "Son of Perfection," as follows:

"When the solar electricity has activated the Pituitary and Pineal glands (in the brain), seeing and hearing blend into a single sense, by which colors and sounds are both seen and heard.

"That is the function of the sixth and seventh sense powers which rise above the time-space element; and so Apollonius, while preaching in Ephesus, saw the assassination of the tyrant Domitian in Rome, many miles away" (Part II, p. 1).

* * * * * * * * * * *

Chapter No. 27

THE MYSTIC SLEEP

When the church fathers prepared the Bible for the use of the church, they usually presented the fables of the Ancient Masters as factualities.

One of these is the fable of the Mystic Sleep, where the gospel Jesus is pictured in the startling drama of raising Lazarus from the dead.

The Masters fabulized the process of Birth in the Flesh as the Death and Burial of Solar Man in a physical prison. They said:

"The Soul becomes 'cribbed, cabined, and confined' in the limitations of the carnal body, as it loses a dimension of Consciousness at each step on the descending path. It becomes bound in the sensual and palpable, after previously having had the power to range at will thru limitless space and universal thought."

According to the Masters, when Solar Man descends into the terrestrial temple, on the approach and at the moment of his divulsion from his celestial abode, there ensues an intermediate or preparatory stage, a diminution of Consciousness, termed a swoon.

In the Tibetan Book of the Dead, a rare work which the church failed to find and destroy, the Celestial Man is represented as retrograding step by step into the lower state of Consciousness. Each step downward to incarnation is comparable to falling asleep.

This is the ancient fable of the Mystic Sleep of Solar Man in the dense body. This is the fable from which the church fathers stole the story that Jesus was notified that Lazarus (Ausares) was sick.

Jesus said, "This sickness is not unto death" (Jn. 11:4).

According to the biblical account, an emergency call for help was sent to Jesus, but he calmly tarried "two days still in the same place" (Jn. 11:6).

Then Jesus said, "Lazarus (Ausares) sleepeth; but I go, that I may awake him out of (the mystic) sleep" (Jn . 11:11).

As the fable is presented in the Bible, it has caused the gullible masses to swallow it as freely as children swallow the Santa Claus fable.

AUSARES

When the neophyte was initiated in the Egyptian Mysteries, he was taught the secret of life by being shown the figure of Ausares (Osiris) on its funeral bier. At the head stood Neophythys, and at the foot, Isis, presented in the Bible as the "two sisters of Lazarus," who weep for him.

Hovering over the body was "a dove with outstretched wings" (Budge), which symbolized the Soul, the Ego, leaving the body at death.

This scene was used to teach the neophyte how Celestial Man looks down on Terrestrial Man at death.

Another scene was presented in the Egyptian Mysteries to teach the neophyte how the New rises from the Old, and Paul (Pol) used it in his work. He said, "That which thou sowest is not quickened, except it die" (1 Cor. 15:36).

As the New Life rises from the old grain that is planted, so the New Life rises from the demised body of man.

Planted grain becomes not extinct. In the birth of the New, the material part of the grain disintegrates and returns to cosmic gas. But the Life of the grain goes on.

The dead body never rises from the grave in its organized form, as so falsely presented in the Bible in the case of the gospel Jesus.

Jesus said that Lazarus was not dead but sleeping and needed to be awakened.

The Masters said that the Soul in the body was not dead, but sleeping.

In the Egyptian drama, thousands of years before the world ever heard of the gospel Jesus, the "body" of Ausares (Osiris) was interned in a cave, and Horus "raised" his "dead" father at Anu by calling unto him to rise and come forth.

Thousands of years later, Jesus "cried in a loud voice, "Lazarus (Ausares) come forth" (Jn. 11:43).

When the church fathers presented this Egyptian fable in the Bible, Horus became Jesus, Ausares became Lazarus, Anu became Bethany, and the two sisters became Mary and Martha.

It is man in his body who is really asleep. Paul said: "Awake, thou that sleepest and arise from the dead" (Eph. 5:14).

Again Paul said: "You have the name that you are alive, but you are dead" (Rev. 3:1).

Physical waking consciousness is merely a sleepy form of life. The Ancient Masters called it a form of death. Plotinus declared: "Death to the soul is to descend into matter and be entirely subjected to matter."

The "sleep" of the Soul in the body is the reign of physical man. But there is no actual sleep of the Soul; it is only apparent. For the Life of the body is the Life of the Soul, and the functions of the body are the work of the Soul.

THE BRAIN

One author states that in the wonderful convolutions of the brain we have an image of the Universe.

The great Carrel wrote: "We possess no technique capable of penetrating the mysteries of the brain and of the harmonious association of its cells.

Our mind . . . is bewildered when it contemplates the stupendous mass of cells, humors, and consciousness which make up the individual" (*Man The Unknown*).

Mind and Ego are identical. Man is Mind incarnated. In Oriental philosophy, Mind is called Manas, a word having for its root Man.

Man has a sevenfold nature. The three self-conscious entities in the East called Atma, Buddhi, and Manas, are immortal. The other four are termed Kama-manas (desire mind), Prana (animating principle), Linga-sarira (astral or etheric model body), and Sthula-sarira, or physical body. These last four are mortal.

All are part of the whole man. This composite nature of man involves the concept of Seven Grades of Consciousness, the Sixth Sense being a full, self-conscious immortality, living in the cosmos as a god, until lastly there is acquired perfect self-consciousness, or consciousness of the self; and this becomes the seventh sense.

The three higher (the higher triad) are all separately self-conscious, each one in sequence communicating with and illuminating that inferior to it. The quaternary of four grades of substance intermixed, constituting physical man on earth, each grade with its own rate of vibration, and so permitting various grades of consciousness to operate thru them.

This quaternary represents man as we know him on the earth plane, where he is dominated by a Stream of Consciousness, coming via the Silver Cord from the higher triad.

While on the earth plane, the Real Man dwells in the brain, the rest of the dense body consisting of extensions and expansions of the Real Man.

Many ages ago, when the ancient Yoga system of the Orient was at its height, there existed the Consciousness which causes the Yoga student to say to himself:

"When thou dost inhale the air charged with Prana (solar electricity), when thou dost send this breath of air into thy head, then canst thou comprehend the mysteries of the Universe in the likeness of this universe (the microcosm), in the special extension of the nerve system in thy head."

This was the original Yoga and not that which prevails now in a decadent form.

THE BODY AT DEATH

Do not cremate nor embalm the dead body until at least three days after death because the vital body should be given that much time to free itself entirely from the dense body.

To cremate or embalm the body before that much time has elapsed tends to disintegrate the vital body, which should be kept intact until the panorama of the past life has been etched into the desire body.

* * * * * *

Chapter No. 28

REINCARNATION

In the Tantrik Manual (Shat-Chakra-Nirupanam), a document most difficult to obtain and written in Sanscrit, it is said that the pericarp of the Muladhara chakra is a triangle or Kanda, in which terminates the lower part of the Spinal Cord. Just above it, on a level with the lower end of the spinal canal, the Kundalini (Cosmic) Fire is said to be sleeping, closing the mouth of the Brahmadwara (Sushumna nadi).

(Note: A fuller explanation of these and other ancient secrets appear in our work titled *Son of Perfection* in two parts. - Hotema.)

Extending upward from the sleeping Kundalini, otherwise called Kula-Kundalini, a fiber, described by the Yogins, glitters like a chain of brilliant lights in the cavity of the Muladhara.

From the edges of the dormant Kula-Kundali there starts another Kundalini, which ascends along the Sushumna and reaches to a point (Bindu Shiva) that is bathed in the Nectar Life from the Eternal Bliss (Brahmarandhra), and illuminates by its radiance even the lowest cavity of this bodily universe, the microcosm.

It will thus be seen that Kundalini extends from the brain down to the lowest chakra of the spine (Muladhara) and is divided into dual parts by the Kula-Kundali which rests on the lower end of the spinal canal, the Brahmadwara, or the lower gate of Brahma.

The Kundalini, in the lower gateway of Brahma, is said to be in an inert state, but at the upper gateway of Brahma the "door opened in heaven," it is in an active state capable of being stimulated.

According to Yoga, the Muladhara chakra and the Fonticulus Frontalis define the limits of Kundalini, or the Parameshwari of lives that breathe—that is, the physical body. For the Solar Body does not breathe and may go unharmed thru fire and water.

When the Kula-Kundali is awakened or activated, it "burns" a passage up thru the various Chakras, as we have explained in *Son of Perfection*, inciting them to action; and, as it rises step by step, the Mind becomes stronger and clearer. When it reaches the brain, wonderful visions and peculiar powers come to a Yogi, and the Soul finds itself free in all respects. The Yogi is liberated from his body but still attached to it by the Silver Cord.

Kundalini, called the Mother of the Universe, then joins her Lord Para-Shiva, who has the form of a dot, or O-Bindu-Rupa, the Cosmic Unit composed of the Four Seed Atoms and situated in the medulla oblongata.

Kundalini thus connects herself with Brahma-randhra, or the cavity in the brain where the Brahma (Solar Man) is located and conscious knowledge of which the Yogi seeks to attain.

This cavity (cave) is guarded by five doors, and Kundalini is said to be the only known power that can open them.

It is in this cavity where Prana (solar electricity) centers all its activities; where Solar Man resides; where the unruly Chitta (lower mind) is captured and controlled by the process of Pranayama (certain breathing exercises).

It is here that the Chitta is submerged in Prana, the submersion bringing to rest all the activities of Mind and Prana.

The Chitta is ruled by the five senses; and these are symbolized in the Bible as the "five kings (who) fled and hid in a cave" (Jos. 10:16).

Then Joshua smote the five kings and slew them (Jos. 10:26), and the Soul (Solar Man), thus set free from the thraldom of the five senses, feels its own joy and sees itself "So 'ham" i.e., "I am That," or "I Am He"; literally, "That Am I."

And the Old Testament God told Moses that his name was "I Am That I Am" (Ex. 3:14).

According to Yoga, when the Mind and Prana act as two conflicting entities, they run riot and keep the Soul in the bondage of the Maya (the surrounding objects of the five senses).

CORD OF DESIRE

Max Heindel said, "As long as man entertains the desires connected with earth life, he must stay in his desire body; and as the progress of man requires that he pass on to the higher Regions, the existence of the Desire World must necessarily become purgative, tending to purify him from his binding desires" (*Rosicrucian Cosmo-Conception*, p. 104).

Altho the Soul is freed from the shackles of Chitta and Prana, it is still forced to remain in its physical prison by the current of Vasana (Cord of Desire), which is guarding the orifice of this cavity in the brain.

These desires of the five senses revert the Soul to the control of Chitta and Prana, and the results are successive rebirths (reincarnation).

Reincarnation is the physical prison which the Yogi strives to escape. He wants to be free of the physical world, and that freedom can be gained only by severing the Cord of Desire and bringing Kundalini under conscious control.

When Kundalini is made to obey the callings of the Soul, the Soul then escapes from this cavity and occupies another cavity called Akasha, which surrounds the brain and Spinal Cord, as we have said.

Furthermore, the Soul, when freed from the control of Chitta, Prana, and Vasana, dwells outside of the Sahasrara Chakra, which we have described in *Son of Perfection*, and is said to pervade the whole universe.

When the Yogi has attained this state, he is said to be in the Nirvikalpa Samadhi (Seedless Samadhi), by which he attains complete harmony with the Infinite and escapes from the process of reincarnation.

What are we to understand by the term Vasana which leads man to successive rebirths?

To know the proper meaning of the term, according to Hindu Philosophy, we shall have to deal with Karma of the embodied man, the Jivatma of a being.

Karma of an individual is comprised of desire (Vasana), knowledge (Jnana), and action (Kriya).

The impressions unconsciously left on the mind by actions in past lives (Vasana) start a current of thought, which is conveyed to the Jivatma, and is then translated, thru this agency, into actions, good or evil. Our good actions lead us to happiness, while the evil ones to misery.

Karma is of three kinds. Sanchita Karma, the outcome of Sanskara (impression of antecedent incarnations), and desires (Vasana), is all the accumulated and unexhausted Karma of previous lives with which an individual is born and which is still to bear fruit.

Prarabdha Karma is that part of the Sanchita Karma which is worked out, and the result of which is made known to us in our present life.

Kriyamana Karma, either Vartaman or Agami, is that which a man is continuously conserving by his present and future actions.

It will thus be seen that the vicious circle of Vasana, by continuously weaving a web around the Soul, forces it to remain embodied for liberating and experiencing the past Karma. So, its final emancipation could be achieved only by putting a stop to the generation of new Kara by conquering our Vasana or desires.

When this is done, there is nothing left to generate new Karma, and the Jivatma is liberated from reincarnation.

On the physical plane, this can be done only by controlling the Cord of Desire, the Vagus nerve (Kundalini), by consciously controlling all the involuntary actions of the body which are in some sense or other under the control of the Vagus nerve.

By submersion of the voluntary and involuntary actions of the body into Chitta and Vasana, all the functions of the body are brought to a state of automatism.

Finally, the embodied Soul (Jivatma), being freed from the activities of the body, merges into the Supreme Soul (Paramatma) outside the body and gains its final emancipation, i.e., liberation from reincarnation.

* * * * * * * * * * * *

Chapter No. 29

THE LOST WISDOM

The Secrets of Life contained in this work have been culled with great care from the fragments of ancient philosophy that escaped the destructive hands of the church fathers who founded Roman Catholicism in the fourth century.

81

The struggle for power between the priesthood and the philosophers had grown so fierce by the time Constantine ascended the throne of the Caesars in the early part of the fourth century that he was constrained to take drastic action to end the strife and preserve his empire.

To that end he called what is known as the First Council of Nicea. This was in the year 325 A.D.

In that convention the battle was fought to a finish, with his victory going to the priesthood, and the Roman State Church was founded.

At the conclusion of the convention, Constantine issued an edict that put the priesthood in power and outlawed the philosophers and their work. The Secrets of Life taught by the philosophers were banished from the Empire, and the philosophers were driven into exile.

So far as the masses were concerned, that was the end of the Ancient Wisdom.

Then came the struggle to convert the people to the New Religion and the making of a Bible to back up the claims of the New Religion.

In this Bible the masses were given a God-man, born of a virgin, a Savior, a Son of a mythical God. His life was presented as the acme of ideal perfection, and his power was derived directly from Divinity itself. Then he "died on the cross" to save the sinners from the just penalty of their evil transgressions.

The church fathers knew the stories of Buddha and his incarnations; the myth of Krishna, most popular of the Hindu gods, usually held to be the eighth incarnation of the god Vishu; the illustrious record of Apollonius, whom the people of Asia Minor worshipped as a god; the sacred legends of Osiris, the god and goddess of Egypt.

It was easy to combine all this in the New Testament gospels and to give the world a perfect character in the form of Jesus and, in his name, to unite the religious worship of all the people of the Roman Empire.

And the deceived world has worshipped for centuries at the shrines of a religion that was fabricated by the priesthood from the myths of antiquity.

Little did the Greeks and Romans dream that they and their children, for fifteen hundred years, were fated to see rivers reddened with their blood because of that Jesus, whom they had mocked and ridiculed, while their proud Empire would crumble into darkness as the Roman Hierarchy rose in power and with Bible in one hand and bloody sword in the other, gradually clamped its galling yoke upon the countries controlled by Rome.

SUMMARY

1. The New Religion formulated by the priesthood of Rome in the fourth century is a myth.

2. That religious system was fabricated from the legends of the gods of India, Egypt, Greece, and Asia Minor.

3. The story of Jesus was exerpted from the writings of Damis concerning his master Apollonius, often called Apollo, or the God of the Sun.

4. Damis was a Greek historian of Assyrian birth who lived and wrote in the first century A.D., and he is mentioned twice in the New Testament--Col. 4:14 and 2 Tim. 4:10.

And that, in a few words, is the story of how Christianity was born and Europe plunged into darkness and how the Western World lost The Wisdom of the Ancient Masters.

A NEW UNIVERSE

One who reads this work with understanding has seen a new heaven and a new earth; for the heaven and the earth of the church have vanished along with the sea of illusion.

That man knows he is the Holy City coming down from the sky--from the God in the Silver Cord--made ready as a bride bedecked for her husband.

And for that man, there shall be no more death; for the former things, taught by schools, colleges, and the church have passed away.--Rev. 21:1-4.

In 1689 a nobleman named Casimirus Linzynsky was beheaded on orders of the church for writing a small manuscript in which he said:

"God is not the creator of man, but man is the creator of God. He made a God for himself out of nothing" (Dr. Wall, p. 338).

The church is ever careful to see that man does not discover his own divinity or to appreciate the magnitude of his own station in the world, recited in the Bible as being that of having dominion over the whole earth (Gen. 1:26).

When the despots, in their long struggle, finally were able to crush the Ancient Mystery Schools, then was broken that line of Ancient Wisdom which had existed and extended thru the ages between man and the hidden secret of his own Soul.

The very idea of that Ancient Wisdom gradually grew more dim and more fantastic, diverging more and more from the orthodox view, so that now the Doctrine of Esotericism is opposed to all the accepted opinions of life.

When man has stood in eternity with himself alone, with Time and Space absorbed into his own being, with his true divinity looming before him in splendor inconceivable, he returns to his regular consciousness with a far different understanding of the mystery called Man.

The New Universe, the New Jerusalem coming down from heaven (Rev. 21:1-4) is Man, the Microcosm, whom the Sun, the Moon, and all the Stars of the sky have helped to mould and make.

For in every man, however fallen and degraded, are contained all the forces, both cosmic and deific, which brought him into existence and have nurtured him throughout the ages in countless incarnations upon earth.

And these same creative forces but await the time when the resurgent
Divine Life again stirs within him, and then Man sees a new world and is not
satisfied to go back to the old World of darkness and deceit.

The greatest discovery of modern times has been man's discovery of himself, made possible by curbing the power of the church.

Man is beginning to recognize the face, over the protest of the priests
and preachers, that he possesses all the Powers which he has been taught to
ascribe to a God. That these powers are mutual and latent, awaiting only his
development and not the supernatural acquirement of a future state.

It is encouraging to observe, in the forward march of man to a higher
life, that the press reported church attendance for the year 1956 fell more
than two million below that of 1955.

There was another report in the press of January 1, 1957, which appeared
to indicate the bitterness engendered in the heart of humanity by man's discovery of himself and the manner in which he has been enslaved by the church.

The press on that date reported the burning of two Catholic churches in
Hartford, Conn., one of them being St. Patrick's Catholic Church and the
other, the huge, expensive, historical St. Joseph's Roman Catholic Cathedral.

That is the kind of work that church was doing in the centuries from the
fourth to the tenth, when the priests went with the Roman Armies on their
missions of destruction thru Egypt and Asia Minor, demolishing the Temples
and the Ancient Mystery Schools of the Masters and burning the libraries
which contained the precious scrolls in which was recorded the Wisdom of the
Ancient Masters.

All of which reminds us of that statement in the Bible:
"For they that take the sword shall perish with the sword" (Mat. 26:52).

* * * * *

George R. Clements, LL.B., LIT.D., N.D., D.C. (Professor Hilton Hotema and
the author Klamonti were the pen names of Dr. Clements). He passed away in
his 94th year in Sebring, Florida in 1970.
He first began his climb to fame as a traveling clergyman, later as
Naturopath and Chiropractic doctor. He was a Mason, an accomplished musician,
made violins. His greatest love was research into longevity and philosophy
of life. He was at one time a partner of Herbert M. Shelton, N.D. They
wrote the Correspondence Course on Orthopathy.
Many have maintained that Dr. Clements (Hotema) was a true mystic and
wished to meet him. He received world-wide correspondence. His early child-
hood, life's history, is given in his book, *Long Life in Florida*.